QUIET FAITH

Smyth & Helwys Publishing, Inc.
6316 Peake Road
Macon, Georgia 31210-3960
1-800-747-3016
©2013 by Judson Edwards
All rights reserved.
Printed in the United States of America.

The paper used in this publication meets the minimum requirements of
American National Standard for Information Sciences—
Permanence of Paper for Printed Library Materials.
ANSI Z39.48–1984. (alk. paper)

Library of Congress Control Number: 2013940979

# Quiet Faith

## An Introvert's

## Guide to

## Spiritual Survival

Judson Edwards

For Nicholas and Abram,
who make me proud

# Contents

# Introduction

I love to browse at bookstores. I can think of few activities more enjoyable than wandering through a bookstore, coffee in hand, looking for a book that just might provide me hours of delight. I've discovered countless literary treasures on previous meanderings through bookstores, so I'm always hopeful as I browse.

The problem I now face is the problem all book lovers and book browsers face: bookstores are vanishing from the face of the earth. There was a time when I had several little "mom-and-pop" bookstores where I could shop—eccentric, out-of-the-way places full of character and personality. But they have gradually closed, one by one, and now I have two main options close to my house: Barnes & Noble or Barnes & Noble.

So I often go to one of those big bookstores and spend a couple of hours browsing. Or I browse online at Amazon, which is easier and handier but not nearly as much fun as actually going to a real store and touching and smelling real books.

But whether I'm combing the shelves at Barnes & Noble or browsing online at Amazon, I am focused on the same delightful task: finding a book that will become a friend. I have many such friends in my study at home and feel comforted and rejuvenated in their presence. These friends have entertained me, instructed me, and given me joy when I needed it most. My life is richer because of them.

What I am always trying to find, of course, is that book written specifically for me. I know they are out there if only I can find them. They address *my* needs, answer *my* questions, have *my* kind of humor, and are written in *my* kind of style. It's as if the book should have stamped on its cover, *Written especially for Judson Edwards*. But because I have yet to see that message stamped on any book, I have to try to determine for myself if a book has my name on it.

It is entirely possible that you are involved in such a search yourself. You are looking at this book, wondering if it has your name on it, wondering if it addresses your needs and questions, wondering if it's worth the price someone is asking you to pay for it.

Perhaps I can help you decide. Let me ask you some questions, and then you might be able to determine if this book is for you.

• Do you ever feel out of step with contemporary American Christianity? Do you yearn for a quieter, more reflective way of experiencing God?

• Do you ever think that we Christians have somehow lost our way and have started majoring on minors? Would you like to recover the essence of the Christian Way?

• Do you cringe at the thought of evangelizing anyone? Does the prospect of having to sell Jesus to your family and friends fill you with dread?

• Do you sometimes wonder if God speaks to people today? More to the point, do you sometimes wonder if God speaks to *you*?

• Do you feel that the church is as much a hindrance as a help to your relationship with God? Are you frustrated by the conflict, pettiness, and bureaucracy in most churches?

• Do you at least occasionally have doubts about what you have always been taught about God? Do you have major questions about God and the Bible that you can't mention to your Christian friends?

• Are you very different from most other Christians? Do you sometimes wonder if you even believe in the same God those Christians believe in?

• Would you like a quiet faith that is uniquely yours, a faith that is honest and real, a faith that gives you joy and sees you through the hard times you have to face?

If your answer is "yes" to most of those questions, this book might become one of your friends.

In the pages to come, I will try to answer those questions for myself and hope that you will be stimulated and helped by my thoughts. Even if you don't agree with all of my conclusions, perhaps you will be provoked to come up with some of your own. I plan to ask, seek, and knock and see what happens. I invite you to join me as we consider together how to forge a quiet faith in a world of hustle and hype.

If we are honest and persistent enough, perhaps Someone will answer the door and bless us with truth.

# CHAPTER 1

# Confessions of a Quiet Christian

*(Has the Whole World Gone Crazy?)*

The event I'm going to tell you about happened more than twenty years ago, but I remember it as if it happened yesterday.

A nationally known men's conference was scheduled to come to Houston, where I was a pastor at the time, and some of the men in our church wanted to attend. They wanted me to attend, too, so one of them paid my way to go to the conference. On the appointed night, a group of ten or twelve of us got on our church bus and headed for the Astrodome.

The Dome was teeming with perhaps 40,000 Christian men. The evening is a blur in my memory, and there is much about it that I have mercifully forgotten, but I do remember some things. It was crowded, loud, and chaotic. It's probably impossible for 40,000 men to do anything quietly, and this conference bore that out. We jostled with thousands of men in the hallways, sat shoulder to shoulder with strangers in our cushioned seats, heard blaring Christian music, and listened to boisterous, energetic preaching.

We had a prayer time where we were asked to pray with the men around us. We were told to pray in groups of four, with one person praying until a bell rang, and then it was the next person's turn to pray. I remember feeling awkward about praying with strangers and shocked when, in the middle of my prayer, the bell rang. I stopped mid-sentence, and the man to my right started his prayer.

At some point during the evening, our host announced that, at the end of the service, all pastors would be invited to come to the front where men who were members of their church would "lay hands on them" and offer them words of encouragement. I remember feeling terrified by the possibility. Did I really want to go forward and have hands laid on me? Did I really want the men in our church feeling obligated to participate in such an event? The answers were "no" and "no," so I did the only logical thing I could think of: I left.

Shortly after that announcement, I got up from my seat and wandered the halls of the Astrodome, feeling very alone. Why was I the only one in this throng of men "turned off" by the proceedings of the conference? What was wrong with me? This seemed to be a spiritual mountaintop for most of the men present, but for me it was sheer misery. Did I have a problem, or was it possible that the whole world had gone crazy, and I was the only sane person left?

Eventually, I rejoined our group (but I refused to go forward and have hands laid on me), and we got on our bus and went back to the church. To say that evening was not a spiritual mountaintop for me would be greatly understating the case. It was an evening I have spent twenty years trying to forget.

## Analyzing the Experience

As I analyzed my experience that night at the Astrodome, I recognized several facets of the conference that prompted my misery.

First, it was too big and noisy for me. I have never liked crowds, and I have never liked noise, and I had them both in spades that evening. I wonder if it's even possible for a person with my temperament to experience God in a crowd of 40,000 people. I seem to have trouble hearing the still, small voice of God when the crowd numbers more than one.

Second, the idea of praying until the bell rang seemed ludicrous to me. How can anyone think about God and enter into the quiet presence of God when a clanging bell is about to sound? How can anyone possibly hear God in a din of noise punctuated by ringing bells? Once again, I have trouble praying when more than one person gets in the prayer closet.

Third, the notion of orchestrating encouragement by having pastors come to the front and having hands laid on them seemed meaningless to me. If someone is commanded to show love and support, how genuine is that love and support? Isn't orchestrated love an oxymoron? If I am asked to be the recipient of such a show of support, I think I'll pass. Forced intimacy is no intimacy at all.

But then again, that's just me. I have to acknowledge that for many (most?) of the men at the Dome that evening, the conference met a real need in their lives and inspired them to be better men. At least from all the indications I could see, I was the oddball at the conference. I was the introvert who didn't like crowds, the skeptic who didn't want to pray, and the loner who refused to receive the encouragement of his friends.

As we boarded our bus to go back to our church, I assumed one of two things had to be true. Either I was indeed a misfit sorely in need of a personality overhaul, or the rest of the world—or at least the evangelical branch of it on display in the Astrodome that evening—had gone completely crazy.

I wanted to think the latter was true, but I feared the problem was with me. I boarded our bus thinking that I needed either a personality overhaul or spiritual renewal—or both.

## Can a Friendly Person Like Me Be an Introvert?

Eventually, I made peace with that experience and concluded that neither I nor the other 39,999 men in the Dome that night were wrong. In truth, the other 39,999 men at the conference were to be commended for being there and for wanting to strengthen their relationship to God.

And, in truth, I didn't need either a personality overhaul or a spiritual renewal; I just needed to come to grips with the way I'm "wired." That night in the Dome—and dozens of similar experiences—made me face again the dreaded "I" word. As a pastor and leader, I hated to acknowledge that I was a full-fledged, card-carrying introvert.

Most of the people in my church would have thought that unlikely. After all, I stood in front of large crowds Sunday after Sunday to preach sermons. I stood in the foyer after every worship service, shaking hands with worshipers and greeting guests with genuine warmth. I visited sick people in hospitals and old people in retirement centers. I performed weddings and funerals just about every week. And, occasionally, I stood in front of large groups playing the guitar and belting out tunes. Almost daily, I was out there among people or on stage in front of people, and most observers would have dubbed me a gregarious extrovert.

But not my wife. Not my kids. Not my parents. And not even my closest friends in the church. They all knew that those activities drained me. They knew that I could perform before the crowd for a while, but I really thrived when I was alone—reading a book, running my miles through the neighborhood, or at the coffee shop working on my own writing. They knew—and I knew it too—that I am really an introvert.

In her book, *Quiet*, Susan Cain devotes an entire chapter to introverts who are forced by their roles to be extroverts. She says it is a common practice and that "introverts are capable of acting like extroverts for the sake of work they consider important, people they love, or anything they value highly."[1]

That was me for thirty-eight years: an introvert in extrovert's clothing, doing the work of a pastor for the sake of work I considered important, people I loved, and a gospel I valued highly.

Not long ago, I read Adam McHugh's book *Introverts in the Church*, and confirmed what I suspected: I am even more of an introvert than I thought. In the book, he lists the following common attributes of introverts:

• Prefer to relax alone or with a few close friends
• Consider only deep relationships as friends
• Need rest after outside activities, even ones we enjoy
• Often listen but talk a lot about topics of importance to us
• Appear calm and self-contained and like to observe
• Tend to think before we speak or act
• May prefer a quiet atmosphere
• Experience our minds going blank in groups or under pressure
• Don't like feeling rushed
• Have great powers of concentration
• Dislike small talk

- Are territorial—desire private space and time
- May treat their homes as their sanctuaries
- Prefer to work on their own rather than with a group
- May prefer written communication
- Do not share private thoughts with many people[2]

Of that list of fifteen attributes of introverts, I have all fifteen of them. Susan Cain has a similar list in *Quiet*, but her list has twenty qualities of introverted people. Again, I have all twenty.

Is it any wonder, then, why I was so miserable at the Dome that night? Like other introverts, I prefer to be alone or with a few friends. I like a quiet atmosphere. I don't like feeling rushed. I prefer to work alone rather than with a group. And I do not share my private thoughts with many people. At that conference, I was a quiet person trying to survive in a loud environment and not having much success.

I've realized through the years that I am not alone in being "wired" that way. Adam McHugh points out that some recent surveys reveal that introverts are actually in the statistical majority at 50.7 percent of the population.[3] Susan Cain says that, depending on the survey, introverts make up between a third and a half of our population.[4]

Regardless of the survey we might quote, though, it is apparent that introverts are not a small minority in our society. What that implies, of course, is that I was probably not the only man in the Astrodome that evening fidgeting in his seat or walking the hallways. Some 20,000 others may have felt the same misery I did.

## Periscope People

When I think about it, I realize I was an introvert even as a child. At the age of about four or five, I received a toy that I still remember as one of my all-time favorites. It was a cardboard periscope, shaped like an "L," and it filled me with joy. I don't remember who gave it to me or what finally became of it, but I do remember being fascinated by it. I carried that periscope with me for days. Of all the toys I received as a child, that is the one I remember best.

That periscope enabled me to see without being seen. I could hide behind a tree, completely hidden from the world, and still observe what was happening. I could squat behind a couch, invisible to my family, and see what everyone else was doing. I could stand behind our wooden backyard fence, poke my periscope into the air, and spy on our next-door neighbors.

That cardboard periscope enabled me to do what all introverts love to do: be invisible while observing and analyzing the world. Introverts are "periscope people," happiest when we can stay on the fringes of life but intensely curious about all that is going on around us.

Sadly, in our culture, we introverts are often seen as people with a problem. We are "loners," "unfriendly," "cold," "misfits," "shy," even "depressed." We live in a world where extroversion is seen as the ideal, and introversion is seen as a problem to overcome.

But it's not just the "world" that values extroversion; the church does, too. Churches are geared for gregarious extroverts, and introverts typically feel uncomfortable and excluded.

If you don't want to shake hands with the person in the pew beside you or witness to your next-door neighbor, what kind of Christian are you, anyway?

If you don't want to stand up and give your testimony in a worship service, why are you so ashamed of the gospel?

If you dread the part of the worship service where you have to mill around the sanctuary greeting guests, why are you so unfriendly?

Really now, why can't you be more like that extroverted, in-your-face apostle named Paul?

Most introverts in the church are convinced they need to become more extroverted to live for Jesus. Conversely, few extroverts feel they need to become more introverted. Perhaps a survey McHugh quotes in his book reveals the reason. That survey revealed that 97 percent of seminary students saw Jesus as an extrovert.[5] If Jesus was an extrovert, doesn't that make extroversion the gold standard for his followers?

But we can no more change our basic personality from introversion to extroversion than we can change our basic eye color from brown to blue. For better or worse, we're stuck with the way we're glued together.

I was reminded of that years ago when I read the books of running "guru" George Sheehan. His books motivated me to start running and to keep running. But they also motivated me to know myself and to be myself.

In his book *Running and Being*, Sheehan wrote about the way he was "glued together":

> When I was young, I knew who I was and tried to become someone else. I was born a loner. I came into this world with an instinct for privacy, a desire for solitude and an aversion to loud voices, slamming doors and to my fellow man. I was born with the dread that someone would punch me in the nose or, even worse, put his arm around me. But I refused to be that person. I wanted to belong. Wanted to become part of the herd, any herd. When you are shy and tense and self-conscious, when you are thin and scrawny and have an overbite and a nose that takes up about one third of your body surface, you want friends, you want to join with others. My problem was not with individuality, but identity. I was more of an individual than I could handle. I had to identify with a group.[6]

Those are the words of a true introvert, a "periscope person" who would like to look at the world from a distance without being noticed. But please understand that we "periscope people" are not all loners, unfriendly, cold, misfits, or depressed. We're just people who enjoy being alone and find that being alone energizes us and restores our sanity.

In fact, I think that's the primary difference between extroverts and introverts. Extroverts get their battery recharged by being around people; introverts get their battery recharged by being alone. It's not that one way is right and the other way is wrong; it's just that people are "wired" differently, and we need to have enough self-awareness to know how *we* happen to be "wired."

## The Power of Introverts

Susan Cain wrote in defense of introverts. Her subtitle to *Quiet* says it all: *The Power of Introverts in a World that Can't Stop Talking*. The world needs introverts, and so does the church. In a world that so rewards and values extroverts, we dare not forget all of the fine things introverts bring to the table.

Adam McHugh mentions several of them in *Introverts in the Church*:

• *Compassion*. Don't mistake our distance there behind our periscope as indifference. We introverts are often compassionate people. We don't gravitate toward masses of people, but we feel deeply about the people we know and love. If you want genuine compassion, "periscope people" are hard to beat.

• *Insight*. Back there behind our periscopes we introverts have plenty of time to observe and analyze what is going on around us. Extroverts are often so action-oriented they don't take the time to peer and ponder, but peering and pondering are trademarks of introverts. We like to look, and we like to think things through, so we're likely to have insights extroverts don't have.

• *Listening and giving space*. In a world of hustle and hype, isn't it nice that some folks will leave you alone, let you talk, and take what you have to say seriously? Back there behind our periscopes, that's exactly what we introverts do. We're quiet. We listen. We give you space so you can have freedom and be who you are. We do not want to push anybody or intrude on anybody's privacy. "Live and let live" is our mantra.

• *Creativity*. Being back there behind our periscope gives us introverts not only ample opportunity to think and ponder but also to create. Introverts tend to be creative people. We write books, paint pictures, compose songs, and invent new contraptions. If you want frenetic action, we might not be your cup of tea. But if you want quiet creativity and if you want to venture into new territory, we can probably fill the bill.

• *Loyalty.* Don't assume that our distance implies a lack of loyalty. We introverts might not have as many relationships as our extroverted friends, but the relationships we do have will be important to us. We will hang with you through thick and thin. We will stand by you when your loud, extroverted friends have deserted you and moved on to someone more engaging.

• *Service.* Because we like being offstage, watching the world from our periscope, we have no desire to gain attention or be noticed. Since most service involves quiet, behind-the-scenes activities like visiting the sick, making soup, loving children, or emptying trash cans, we "periscope people" make good servants. We might not make head-lines, but, frankly, that's fine with us.

• *Calming Presence.* If you want excitement and passion, you might want to dial up an extrovert. But if you want someone to calm the storm, bring peace in the midst of conflict, or speak a word of reason in the midst of an emotional battle, we introverts could serve you better. We are the epitome of what family systems expert Edwin Friedman called the "non-anxious presence" that every system needs to survive.[7]

Those seven qualities are needed in both the world and the church, and we "periscope people" are poised and ready to deliver them, if only someone will receive our gifts. We introverts might not have all the qualities needed in the world and the church, but we do have some indispensable ones to offer. Both the world and the church will suffer if our gifts are not recognized and valued.

## Square Pegs in a Round Church

For all of the fine qualities we introverts bring to the table, the truth remains that we are typically viewed as people in need of a personality upgrade. Those of us who are active in church find that to be true especially in the community of faith. We are consistently, though sub-tly and indirectly, reminded that we need to be bolder, louder, and more certain in our faith. If we ever really got filled with the Spirit, the church seems to suggest, we would become extroverts.

As I think back on a long life as a follower of Jesus and thirty-eight years as a pastor of Baptist churches, I realize that I have always been a square peg in a round church. I never quite fit, never had the necessary attributes to be a strong leader, never was a natural "glad-hander," never wanted to evangelize strangers, and never faced conflict and opposition with anything approaching confidence. I wanted to stay in hiding behind my periscope, but my pastoral role kept demanding that I come out of hiding and be seen and heard.

I'm guessing that my struggles are typical of the struggles of introverted church leaders and introverted laypeople everywhere. In an extroverted church culture, we introverts always feel inadequate and incapable.

Somehow I "hung in there" for thirty-eight years, though, spent thirty-three years in the last two churches, and look back on my ministry with gratitude and satisfaction. If nothing else, my ministry is proof that God can occasionally hit a straight lick with a pretty short stick. I am living proof that an introverted person can do at least a passable job of leading the people of God.

As I think about the issues that I struggled with most in my years as a church leader, I can think of several that caused me consistent anxiety:

• *Leadership.* A church member once commented on my "invisible leadership." I think he meant it as a compliment, but I'm not sure. I do know that I never considered myself a strong leader and struggled when I had to get out ahead of the parade.

• *Supervision.* If a staff person was a "self-starter" and competent, he or she loved my supervision—because there was so little of it! If a staff person needed prodding and direction, he or she wondered why I wasn't providing more help. It's not easy to be a "hands-on" supervisor when you're looking through a periscope.

• *Evangelism.* I would no more think of evangelizing the stranger beside me in an airplane than I would think of trying to persuade that stranger to change her hairstyle. I would hope she would let me read my book, even as I let her read hers. Bearing verbal witness for Christ has always been a challenge for me, and I will probe this dilemma further in a coming chapter.

• *Conviction.* The Apostle Paul said, "This I know . . . ." I usually said, "This I think . . . ." Paul, who comes across as an extrovert if ever there was one, was full of conviction and certainty. I tend to be full of doubt and uncertainty. It's much easier to catch fire around the intense passion of someone like Paul than it is to catch fire around the measured reason of someone like me.

• *Conflict.* I hate conflict and have always avoided it. Generally, that served me well as a pastor, but there were a few occasions when avoiding conflict let a problem grow larger than it should have been. A bit of confrontation could have nipped the problem before it got out of control. I learned the hard way that sometimes avoiding conflict can lead to even more conflict.

• *Vision.* I have never been good at formulating long-range plans. One book I often referred to when I was a pastor was a business book titled *The Futility of Long-Range Planning.* I have always focused on today and maybe tomorrow, but I've had little interest in dreaming about the distant future. So, if a church needed a long-range plan or a specific vision for the next ten years, I had little interest in providing that.

• *Action.* As with most introverted "periscope people," I love to read, write, think, observe, and ruminate. Please, though, don't ask me to *do* anything. Don't ask me to leave my comfortable couch, desk, or hammock to move into action. I would rather think than sweat any day.

• *Community.* I can't tell you how many sermons I preached on the importance of *koinonia,* the church's capacity to be a community. I frequently held up the early church as our best example. Those early Christians ate together, prayed together, carried one another's burdens, and even gave away their possessions to provide for one another's needs. "We must be like that," I told our church. "We must be a family." But those admonitions to join together as a family of faith sometimes flew in the face of my true inclinations. Many days, I didn't want community; I wanted privacy. Many days, I wanted to walk away from the family of faith and recover my sanity *alone.*

Susan Cain suggests that introverts actually make better leaders than extroverts. Introverts have a softer, more compassionate, servant-oriented kind of leadership, she says, that enables families, businesses, and churches to thrive. Perhaps she is right. I certainly would like to think so. I only know that my basic temperament and personality were often at odds with what our culture sees as strong leadership. As I said, that I could be the pastor of two churches for thirty-three years is something of a miracle. It speaks to both the mysterious ways of God and the gracious ways of God's people that an "invisible leader" like me could last that long.

## Beyond Equations, Formulas, and Recipes

Our culture loves spiritual equations, formulas, and recipes. That's why we preachers preach sermons titled "Five Ways to Know God," "The Six Secrets of a Successful Marriage," and "Seven Simple Steps to Happiness." We preachers know that if we can reduce God and life to equations, formulas, and recipes, we will always have a ready audience.

But many of us also know that God and life are more complicated than our sermons make them out to be. We know that God and life can't be captured in equations, formulas, and recipes, and that trying to reduce a relationship with God to four spiritual laws is not going to satisfy a person for long. Let's face it: a relationship with God is fraught with mystery, danger, and particularity. And life itself is fraught with those same characteristics.

It's the particularity part of that relationship with God and the particularity part of life itself that I'm trying to underscore in this book. We each have a particular journey to make with God, and no one can prescribe that journey for us.

The conference that changes your life will send me home in frustration. The book that turned my life around will leave you cold. The church that meets your spiritual need will not meet mine. The preacher who stirs my soul will bore you to tears. When it comes to spiritual journeys, we're each an experiment of one. Sheehan writes,

Yet educators, psychologists, theologians, social scientists and philosophers continue to lump us under that great umbrella, Man. Man, they tell us, using "we" and "our" and "us" and other collective words indiscriminately, should, would, will, ought or must do this or that. They try to set up an all-embracing system of ethics and psychology. Tell us how to act and react. Lump the marathoner and the middle linebacker into one composite human being. It doesn't work in sports. It won't work in life. The centuries-old injunction "Know thyself" still applies.[8]

I've been guilty in this chapter of painting with too broad a brush myself. I've blithely referred to extroverts and introverts as if they're all alike, as if they all have the same strengths and weaknesses. In truth, we human being are much more complicated and confounding than that.

After giving her twenty-point checklist for introverts in *Quiet*, Susan Cain comments,

> But even if you answered every single question as an introvert or extrovert, that doesn't mean that your behavior is predictable across all circumstances. We can't say that every introvert is a bookworm or every extrovert wears lampshades at parties any more than we can say that every woman is a natural consensus-builder and every man loves contact sports. As Jung felicitously put it, "There is no such thing as a pure extrovert or pure introvert. Such a man would be in a lunatic asylum."[9]

Each one of us is a complicated, mysterious, one-of-a-kind creation that defies both logic and explanation. Though we share many things in common, we also live in completely different worlds and view the world through completely different eyes.

An old radio program, "Duffy's Tavern," featured a bartender-philosopher named Archie. One of Archie's regular customers was a simple-minded, friendly chap name Finnegan. Often Finnegan would greet Archie with this question: "How are things in the world, Arch?" Archie would invariably reply, "Your world or mine, Finnegan?"

Your world or mine? That's always a pressing, relevant question. Your approach to God or mine? Your style of worship or mine? Your kind of music or mine? Your way of relating to people or mine? We each have to find for ourselves how we are "wired" and how we can best live with joy.

If we decide to live only by expert advice, we, in effect, abandon our own lives. Like young David, we keep trying to put on Saul's armor as we face our giants, but that armor just doesn't fit. Who knew that we could face our giants armed only with a slingshot and a few stones? We dare not assume that someone else's armor, equation, formula, or recipe will be, or has to be, right for us.

We have each been given the awesome task of finding out who we are and what we are here to do. But the map for discovering those truths can be found only in one's own, solitary heart.

## Good Water

I began this chapter by telling you of my experience at a men's conference years ago. I said that I wondered who was crazy—the large crowd of men caught up in the event or me roaming the hallway trying to escape the event.

Perhaps an appropriate way to end this chapter and to answer that question is to consider an old Sufi tale Walter Truett Anderson recounts in his book *Reality Isn't What It Used to Be*.

According to this tale, mankind was warned by a mysterious teacher that all the water in the world was about to disappear and be replaced by different water. This new water, though, would drive people mad.

Everyone ignored the teacher's warning except one man who collected the good water and stored it in a safe place. When the forewarned day arrived, all the streams and wells went dry, and the man began to drink the old water he had saved.

But when he came out among other people, he found that, just as the teacher had predicted, they had all gone mad. The new water changed the way they thought and lived, and they did not even remember that they had been warned that this would happen.

Worst of all, the people thought *he* was crazy. They assumed that they were normal and that *he* was insane. For some time, he continued to drink his own pure water, but eventually his loneliness got to him. He began to feel so lonely that he gave up his water and started drinking the water everyone else was drinking.

The man soon became like all the rest and forgot about what had happened or where the water of sanity was. All the people around him were happy for him and regarded him as a madman who had become sane again.[10]

The lessons of that story are many: We cannot follow the crowd and find pure water. We had better keep whatever pure water we have discovered in our lives. Sometimes the sanest people in the world look crazy to others. It's lonely trying to find and live your own truth. We're all tempted to give up the search and join the "sanity" of the world.

I've thought of a biblical proof text for that old Sufi story. It is Paul's admonition in Romans 12:1: "Do not be conformed to this world, but be transformed by the renewing of your minds . . . ." In essence, Paul reminds us to shun the water of the world, have our minds renewed, and have our lives transformed by drinking the pure water that keeps us sane.

So who was crazy that night in the Dome? Was it those men caught up in the fervor of the conference? Or was it me—walking the halls, feeling left out and unspiritual? Who was drinking the good water?

I have my opinion, of course, and so do you. As I said earlier, I'm not ready to throw stones at any of those men. Perhaps, with their personality and spirituality, that conference nourished their souls. Perhaps what was good water for them was bad water for me.

But of this I am certain: It would be crazy for someone like me to keep drinking that water. It would be crazy to keep going to those kinds of events and expecting to meet God. I've learned how and where that happens for me, and that's what I want to write about in this book. I want to tell you where I have found the good water and see if you have found it there, too.

Of this I am certain, too: Everything in this book is affected and determined by my personality and temperament. Extroverts fond of noise and crowds will probably find my thoughts odd and irrelevant.

But kindred spirits will, perhaps, read this book and whisper a silent prayer of gratitude that someone in the world is as heretical and strange as they are.

If you are one of those, read on.

## For Reflection or Discussion

1. Have you ever attended a Christian event where you felt completely out of place? How did you respond to that situation?

2. Do you consider yourself an introvert or an extrovert? How many of the fifteen attributes of introverts do you have?

3. Is it hard for introverts to thrive in the church? What can we do to make church more hospitable to introverts?

4. Is it possible for an introvert to be an effective leader? Have you ever known an introverted leader who succeeded?

5. Do you ever feel like a Christian misfit, out of step with most others in the church? How do you handle that?

6. Where do you find the "good water"? How do you renew your soul?

### NOTES

1. Susan Cain, *Quiet* (New York: Crown, 2012) 209.

2. Adam McHugh, *Introverts in the Church*, digital version (Downers Grove IL: Inter-Varsity Press, 2009) location 383.

3. Ibid., location 124.

4. Cain, *Quiet*, 3.

5. McHugh, *Introverts in the Church*, location 106.

6. George Sheehan, *Running and Being* (New York: Warner, 1978) 26.

7. McHugh, *Introverts in the Church*, location 974.

8. Sheehan, *Running and Being*, 29.

9. Cain, *Quiet*, 14.

10. As told in Walter Truett Anderson, *Reality Isn't What It Used to Be* (San Francisco: HarperSanFrancisco, 1990) 217.

# CHAPTER 2

# Reclaiming the Center

*(What's It All About, Anyway?)*

In Gabriel Garcia Marquez's book *One Hundred Years of Solitude*, the people in the village of Macondo begin to lose their memory. To assure that they don't forget some of the most significant things in their lives, they decide to make signs and post them around the village. Among other reminders, they write MACONDO so they won't forget where they live, and they write GOD EXISTS so they won't forget their creator.

I often have the feeling that we modern Christians have taken up residence in Macondo. The only difference is that we don't know that we are losing our memory, so we don't do anything to remember the things that matter. Perhaps we need to post some signs in our houses and churches that remind us of the essential truths we dare not forget.

The result of our amnesia is spiritual vertigo: we are spinning around without any center, without any clear direction to our lives, without any sense of what matters or where we are going.

We have stumbled into the life Yeats described in "The Second Coming":

Turning and turning in the widening gyre
The falcon cannot hear the falconer;
Things fall apart; the centre cannot hold;
Mere anarchy is loosed upon the world,
The blood-dimmed tide is loosed, and everywhere

> The ceremony of innocence is drowned;
> The best lack all conviction, while the worst
> Are full of passionate intensity.[1]

Things both individually and nationally are falling apart because we've lost the center. Like the people of Macondo, we're forgetting essential things, only we don't know it. Or if we do know it, we're not quite sure how to get back to the center.

Certainly, those of us who are Christian never intended to lose the center of our faith. We thought we knew and treasured the key truths that hold our faith together. But I think what happened was insidious and silent: a bunch of good causes and movements attacked the church like a host of computer viruses. They looked like benign, even friendly viruses at first, but they quietly destroyed our center, sent us spiraling into contentious confusion, and made even the finest among us "lack all conviction."

Perhaps a personal illustration can describe what I think has happened to us. Several years ago, my daughter and her husband had to get rid of some bamboo growing in their backyard. The bamboo had been planted to serve as a sound wall for the road noise on the freeway behind them. Their house was located on "Mo-Pac," a heavily traveled road through Austin, and they got a lot of noise from the traffic there. So the bamboo was planted to be a cheap way to block out that noise.

At least, that was the plan. But the bamboo grew . . . and grew . . . and grew, until it completely took over their backyard. My daughter and her husband finally had to enter their bamboo jungle one morning and start hacking away at it to keep it at bay. What seemed like a good idea for a sound wall became an out-of-control "virus" that completely overtook their yard.

Something like that has happened in the church. We started considering "important issues" like biblical authority, abortion, homosexuality, the environment, the role of women in the church, the kind of music we would have in our worship services, and at least a dozen others, and those issues became the "bamboo" that took over the church. Those became our fundamental concerns, our center.

But those issues—as important and relevant as they are—are not our center at all. They will eventually fade into the background only to be replaced by other bamboo issues. If we focus primarily on those concerns, things will fall apart, the center will not hold, and anarchy will be loosed upon the church and the world. And many of us who have been in church all our lives will grow weary of fighting over bamboo issues and decide that church is not worth the hassle.

So we need to remember and reclaim our center—especially those of us who are introverts, who are prone to brood and grow cynical. We need to ask, "What it's all about, anyway? What is the heart of our gospel, the essence of a life with God?" We need to be able to recognize bamboo when we see it and not let it take over our minds and our churches.

What I hope to do in this chapter is think through those questions with you. What *is* the heart of our gospel, and what *is* the essence of a life with God? If we could answer those questions, wouldn't it clarify our calling, maybe even renew our passion? I think it would, and I hope these words will move us in that direction.

I want to look at two verses in Ephesians as we think about those questions. Ephesians 2:8-9 are familiar verses to most of us who have grown up in the church and are conversant with Scripture: "For by grace you have been saved through faith, and this is not your own doing; it is the gift of God—not the result of works, so that no one may boast."

I know there are other verses we could consider as we try to track down the heart of our life in Christ. I know it is foolish to pick out two verses and make them carry the freight of the entire Bible. I also know that, given the opportunity to pinpoint two essential biblical verses, you might go in a completely different direction.

But, for me at least, Ephesians 2:8-9 is a good starting point. These two verses spell out the heart of our gospel and the essence of our journey with God. So, in the spirit of those Macondo villagers, let me post a few signs from these verses that can remind us of important and essential truths. If we choose not to post them in our houses and church sanctuaries, perhaps we can at least post them in our minds.

# GRACE

*"For by grace you have been saved . . . ."*

The first word in the Christian vocabulary is the word "grace." We are saved, the Apostle Paul says, by grace. We begin our life with God by grace, are sustained throughout life by grace, and will one day be welcomed home in eternity by grace. Grace rules, from beginning to end.

What, exactly, does this mean? What is a life of grace? In the memorable words of Robert Capon, "The life of grace is the life of a cripple on an escalator."[2]

That definition has two parts. First, we are all, to use Capon's word, "crippled." In terms of our relationship with God, making it with God, or securing our salvation with God, we are totally crippled. We cannot walk, so we cannot get there. We cannot attend enough worship services, be a wise enough parent, give enough money to the church, build enough Habitat houses, suffer through enough boring sermons, serve on enough church committees, witness to enough secular friends, empty enough bedpans, or go on enough mission trips to make it with God. We are crippled—period. Our finest efforts to climb the ladder to God are destined to end in frustration. "All have sinned and fall short of the glory of God" (Rom 6:23).

Second, there is an escalator that enables us to go where we want to go. Amazingly, God has put us on the escalator that is Jesus and taken us to what the biblical writers call "eternal life." Not because we deserve it. Not because we earned enough brownie points to get it. And not because we finally got our theology right. No, God put us on the escalator that is Jesus because God is full of love and mercy and decided to reconcile the whole world to himself. We got put on the escalator because of who God is, not because of who we are.

Of course, we don't have to believe that. We can continue to act like there is no escalator, that Jesus never lived, died, and rose again, but that doesn't change the plain truth of the gospel: "All this is from God, who reconciled us to himself through Christ, and has given us the ministry of reconciliation; that is, in Christ God was reconciling the world to himself, not counting their trespasses against them, and entrusting the message of reconciliation to us" (2 Cor 5:18-19).

Through Christ, God reconciled the whole world to himself. Our part is to know that, celebrate that, and live in gratitude for that. We are to live every day buoyed and fortified by the incredible message of 1 John 4:19: "We love because he first loved us." We also write, preach, give, worship, serve, and evangelize because he first loved us. We are cripples, placed on the escalator by One who loves us, and we simply can't believe that we could be so blessed.

At least, that's the way it is *supposed* to be. In truth, we are hesitant and skeptical when it comes to grace. Nothing in our experience has prepared us for it. Not school. Not sports. Not business. Not the military. And, sadly, not even the church. In all of those arenas of life, the motto is the same: "You get what you deserve. You pull your own weight. You rise and fall on your own efforts."

So grace seems strange and unlikely. We just can't believe that the good news could be that good, so we go back to the law. Back to pulling our own weight and climbing the ladder of good works. Back to religion with all of its offerings, sacrifices, customs, and traditions. In Paul's packed phrase to the Galatians, we "have fallen away from grace" (Gal 5:3).

Hear Capon again as he writes about our tendency to prefer law to grace:

> Restore to us, Preacher, the comfort of merit and demerit. Prove for us that there is at least something we can do, that we are still, at whatever dim recess of our nature, the masters of our relationships. Tell us, Prophet, that in spite of all our nights of losing, there will yet be one redeeming card of our very own to fill the inside straight we have so long and so earnestly tried to draw to. But do not preach us grace. . . . Give us something, anything; but spare us the indignity of this indiscriminate acceptance.[3]

That is why we need to post the GRACE sign everywhere we can. It is the first word of the Christian experience, and the first word we are prone to forget. Without it, the good news is simply not good. If Christianity is about doing better, working harder, becoming purer, and impressing God with our efforts, it is neither good nor news. If Christianity is those things, it is a religion, just like other religions, and religion is, quite frankly, bad news.

But the Christian gospel is the announcement of the end of religion. We don't have to climb that ladder of works anymore. We're cripples, placed on the escalator by the grace of God, and the best thing we can do is enjoy the ride and celebrate all the way to the top.

We need to post the GRACE sign in a prominent place and look at it often. Knowing and remembering grace will infuse us with joy and change the way we live.

## FAITH

*". . . . through faith . . . ."*

We are saved, Paul says, by grace through faith. We have to have enough faith to believe that God has reconciled us to himself in Christ. We have to have enough faith to believe that the good news is as good as it claims to be. Grace becomes operative in our experience only when we appropriate it by faith. Think of faith, perhaps, as plugging the grace of God into our souls.

But whether I plug grace into my soul or not, grace is still real. The cross *did* happen. The whole world *has* been reconciled to God. God *did* so love the world. The reconciliation *is* historical fact.

In another of his books, Capon has an illustration that gets to the heart of the meaning of "faith."

> Suppose I were to tell you that I had already buried, under a flat rock on a piece of property you own, $1,000,000 in crisp, new $1,000 bills. And suppose I were to tell you that I have no intention of ever taking this money back; it's there, and that's that.
>
> On one level, I have given you a piece of sensationally good news: you are the possessor of a million bucks, no conditions attached, no danger of my reneging on the gift. And if you trust me—that is, if you go to your property and start turning over flat rocks—you will sooner or later actually be able to relate to the million I so kindly gave you.
>
> But note something crucial. Your faith (your trust) does not earn you the money, nor does it con me into giving it to you: the

money was yours all along just because I was crazy enough to bury it in your backyard. Your faith, you see, in no way is the *cause* of the gift; the only thing it can possibly have any causal connection with is *your own enjoyment of the gift.*[4]

In other words, our faith in no way causes God to love or accept us. Our faith acknowledges that God has already loved and accepted us in Christ. Faith in no way activates the escalator; it just allows us to get on board.

And faith also prompts us to live in new and different ways. Once we plug grace into our souls, we get energized and realize that life on the escalator is quite an adventure. We look at the world with new eyes. As Paul put it to the Corinthians, "So if anyone is in Christ, there is a new creation: everything old has passed away; see everything has become new!" (2 Cor 5:17).

There on the escalator we notice a bunch of other cripples riding with us and decide to form a community with them. There on the escalator we also see host of people who haven't gotten on the escalator and try to encourage them to get on board. There on the escalator we notice some people who are wounded and hurting, and we do what we can to help them. And all the while, we're celebrating the fact that we're on the escalator and rejoicing in the fact that we're held in awfully good Hands.

We need to post the FAITH sign right there beside the GRACE sign. Grace is the incredible love and acceptance of God. Faith is our willingness to believe in that love and acceptance and to plug grace into our experience.

Grace *without* faith is like a live wire that hasn't been plugged in to anything. Grace *with* faith unleashes incredible power.

# GRATITUDE

*". . . . and this is not your own doing; it is the gift of God . . . ."*
Grace is the incredible love and acceptance of God. Faith is plugging that grace and acceptance into our lives. And then comes the gratitude that we ever received these gifts in the first place. Grace is a gift from God. Even the faith to receive and appropriate that grace, Paul says,

is a gift from God. So we receive these gifts and then live out a life of gratitude for them.

Grace, faith, and gratitude: three logical, sequential pieces in the puzzle of our journey with God.

Christina Rossetti once wrote, "Were there no God, we would be in this glorious world with grateful hearts, and no one to thank."[5] But we Christians do have someone to thank, so we spend our days living in gratitude and expressing our thanks to God.

If we get spiritually mature enough, we live in gratitude even when life is hard and the world gets heavy. Though it is not easy, we learn to live out Paul's admonition to give thanks *in everything*.

When John Claypool was pastor of the Crescent Hill Baptist Church in Louisville, Kentucky, over forty years ago, his young daughter, Laura Lue, died of leukemia. After her death, Claypool preached a sermon at Crescent Hill titled "Life Is a Gift."

In that sermon, he told a story about an old, green Bendix washing machine that his family once had when he was a boy. The washing machine actually belonged to a young couple his family knew, but, when the husband was drafted in World War II, and his wife prepared to go with him, they let the Claypools use their old Bendix until they returned.

John Claypool said he grew quite fond of that old washing machine, and, when the war ended and the couple returned to claim their washer, he expressed his displeasure to his mother. Wise woman that she was, she reminded him that the washing machine never belonged to them in the first place and that they got to use it at all was a gift. She told him to use the occasion to be grateful that they ever had the washing machine at all.

Then, after telling that story, Claypool drove home his point:

> Here, in a nutshell, is what it means to understand something as a gift and to handle it with gratitude, a perspective biblical religion puts around all of life. And I am here to testify that this is the only way down from the Mountain of Loss. I do not mean to say that such a perspective makes things easy, for it does not. But at least it makes things bearable when I remember that Laura Lue was a gift,

pure and simple, something I neither earned nor deserved nor had a right to. And when I remember that the appropriate response to a gift, even when it is taken away, is gratitude, then I am better able to try and thank God that I was ever given her in the first place.[6]

I think he's right: gratitude is the only way down from the Mountain of Loss. Unless we can be grateful that we ever had our child in the first place, her death will crush us. Unless we can be grateful that we had years of marriage that produced great kids, the divorce will destroy us. Unless we can lie on our deathbed and be grateful for all the blessings we have received, our death will terrify us.

Gratitude really is the only way down from any loss or tragedy we experience. Without gratitude, our lives are destined to be filled with regret and sadness.

But with gratitude, everything changes for the better. Scientists have even started to notice the difference gratitude makes in our lives. Researchers from the University of California at Davis and the University of Miami did a study in which they assigned participants to one of three groups.

The first group was instructed to pay attention to and keep track of daily hassles, annoyances, and irritants. The second group was told to pay attention to experiences they could be grateful for and to keep a record of them. The third group was the control group, told to keep track of neutral life events. All of the participants also were told to keep track of their moods, the time they spent sleeping, and the time they spent exercising.

The study found that the gratitude group was 25 percent happier than the hassle/annoyance group. The gratitude group also reported more optimism and spent more time exercising than the other two groups. The researchers, Robert Emmons and Michael McCullough, concluded, "Results suggest that a conscious focus on blessings may have emotional and interpersonal benefits."[7]

"A conscious focus on blessings" is the consistent invitation of Scripture, and, once we learn to do that, we not only get emotional and interpersonal benefits but also get to climb down from all the Mountains of Loss we have had to scale. We get to replace regret and resentment with joy and contentment. So, right there beside the GRACE and FAITH signs, we post the GRATITUDE sign.

A life with God starts with grace, which we appropriate by faith, which we then live out in the world with gratitude, and which then manifests itself in humility.

## HUMILITY

*". . . not the result of works, so that no one may boast."*

The first three signs I've posted probably don't surprise anyone. Grace, faith, and gratitude are commonly recognized as key ingredients in the Christian life. The fourth sign I want to post—HUMILITY—is not as universally recognized as the other three, but I think it is crucial to a life of joy and purpose.

Humility commends itself to us for two primary reasons. First, it is honest. Humility prevents us from being hypocrites, the primary quality Jesus couldn't tolerate in the Pharisees. The truth is that we all have plenty to be humble about, and we might as well admit it.

When I was in the seventh grade, I took an industrial arts class. Everyone in the class had to make a small, wooden shelf in the shape of Texas. I measured, sawed, and sandpapered to the best of my ability, but my pitiful shelf bore little resemblance to Texas. Mr. Bayh, our teacher, walked by one day as I was working, watched me for a few minutes, and then commented, "You know, Jud, I think you have quite a few talents, but I'm not sure woodworking is one of them."

As painful as it was to hear that, Mr. Bayh was right. When it comes to working with wood, repairing automobiles, painting pictures, operating computers, doing mathematic equations, playing the violin, and a host of other skills too numerous to mention, I have plenty of reasons to be humble. And I'm guessing you have a similar list. Our humility is just an honest recognition of our ignorance and shortcomings.

There is a verse in the Bible that is often called "the great confession." It is Peter's statement to Jesus, "You are the Messiah, the son of the living God" (Matt 16:16). But the second greatest confession in Scripture might be the one Paul and Barnabas make in the book of

Acts. The people in Lystra wanted to declare Paul and Barnabas gods, but they wanted no part of that: "Friends, why are you doing this? We are mortals just like you . . ." (Acts 14:15a).

That was a confession of humanity and humility, and it was an honest admission of reality. Paul and Barnabas knew they weren't gods, so why pretend to be something they were not? Paul would later write to the Romans and say, "Do not think of yourself more highly than you ought to think, but think with sober judgment, each according to the measure of faith God has assigned" (Rom 12:3). He could say that with integrity because he had lived it. Humility is crucial because it enables us to be honest.

Second, humility allows us to serve other people. People striving to be "big shots" are not known for serving other people. The only way to serve anyone is to get *beneath* that person. Trying to serve "from above," from a stance of superiority, just doesn't work. Our attempts to serve "from above" come across as what they really are: attempts to make ourselves look like impressive servants. But real servanthood walks alongside, or gets underneath, and serves from the bottom up. Servant power doesn't trickle down; it trickles up.

Jesus tried to get his disciples to understand that trickle-up kind of power, but they just couldn't comprehend it. They wanted to sit on his right hand and left hand and exert the kind of power that trickles down. So Jesus said to them, "Whoever wants to be first must be last of all and servant of all" (Mark 9:35b).

It's not about being on top; it's about being on bottom. It's not about lording it over other people; it's about not thinking of yourself more highly than you ought to think. It's not about being impressive; it's about being humble so you can serve.

In his book *A Long Obedience in the Same Direction*, Eugene Peterson gives us a fine definition of how a humble person approaches life: "I will not try to run my own life or the lives of others; that is God's business. I will not pretend to invent the meaning of the universe; I will accept what God has shown its meaning to be. I will not noisily strut about demanding that I be treated as the center of my family or my neighborhood or my work, but seek to discover where I fit and what I am good at."[8]

## The Beholding Business

In her fine book *Leaving Church*, Barbara Brown Taylor describes the growing disillusionment she felt as she served as pastor of an Episcopal church in Georgia:

> I had become an Episcopalian in the first place because the Anglican way cared more for common prayer than for right belief, but under stress even Episcopalians began vetting one another on the virgin birth, the divinity of Jesus, and his physical resurrection from the dead. Both in Clarksville and elsewhere, the poets began drifting away from churches as the jurists grew louder and more insistent. I began to feel like a defense attorney for those who could not square their love of God with the Nicene Creed, while my flagging attempt to be all things to all people was turning into a bad case of amnesia about my own Christian identity.
>
> My role and my soul were eating each other alive. I wanted out of the belief business and back into the beholding business. I wanted to recover the kind of faith that has nothing to do with being sure what I believe and everything to do with trusting God to catch me though I am not sure of anything.[9]

I find myself saying a loud "Amen" to those words. Like her, I fear the poets are getting sick and tired of the church's bickering and quietly slipping out the back door. Like her, I often felt that my role and my soul were eating each other alive when I was a pastor. And, like her, I long to get out of "the belief business" and back into "the beholding business."

I have no desire anymore (if I ever did) to argue theology with anyone. If you want to hold a contentious church meeting to debate the divinity of Jesus, the authority of the Bible, what Scripture says about homosexuality, or any of the other "bamboo" issues invading the church today, I will go a-fishing. It's not that those are unimportant topics; it's just that time is short for me, and I want to focus on the truths that will keep me alive and joyful.

When I come to your church, tell me, please, about grace. Remind me, in a world of push-and-shove and climb-your-way-up-the-ladder that God has done something incredible for me in Christ.

Remind me that I am the prodigal son who got the party even though I don't deserve it, and the worker in the vineyard who showed up at quitting time and got the whole day's pay.

And remind me about faith. Tell me to plug this grace into my life and to keep believing it even though it seems illogical and unreasonable. Keep telling me to have faith in the gracious goodness of God, so that I will be motivated to serve and love and give as I should.

Tell me, too, about gratitude. Preach to me the story of Zacchaeus, who was so moved by the grace of Jesus that he became a grateful giver. Keep giving me the picture of that crazy Apostle Paul, singing from a prison cell, "I have learned to be content with whatever I have" (Phil 4:11b). Keep telling me of gratitude so I can come down from all of my Mountains of Loss.

Please remind me to practice humility, so that I can be honest and so that I can serve others. Keep telling me that God is God, that the world doesn't revolve around me, that I am too sinful to throw stones at anyone else, and that a big ego is a sign that I don't know God.

Those are the four things I want to remember—GRACE, FAITH, GRATITUDE, and HUMILITY. If I can remember those four essentials, I can keep my relationship with God alive and current. On those four pillars, I can build not only a sound theology but also a life of joy and purpose. As an introvert tempted to brood and become cynical, I need those four foundational truths to keep me focused on the good news of the gospel.

## For Reflection or Discussion

1. Have we modern Christians taken up residence in Macondo? Have we lost the essence of the gospel?

2. Which bamboo issues do you think have most invaded the church and choked out its focus? What can we do about that?

3. The author mentions four words that form the essence of his faith. What words capture the essence of your faith? What truths do you consider essential?

4. Do you believe that God has already reconciled the world through Christ? What do we have to do to activate that reconciliation?

5. What are you especially grateful for? Do you believe that gratitude is "the only way down from the Mountain of Loss"?

6. How can we get more "trickle-up" power in our lives?

7. Have you ever longed to get out of the "belief business" and into the "beholding business"? Do you think that the poets are drifting away from churches?

## NOTES

1. William Butler Yeats, "The Second Coming," in Richard Finneran, ed., *The Poems of W. B. Yeats: A New Edition* (New York: Macmillan, 1924) 187.

2. Robert Farrar Capon, *Between Noon and Three* (San Francisco: HarperSanFrancisco, 1982) 176.

3. Ibid., 8.

4. Robert Farrar Capon, *The Mystery of Christ & Why We Don't Get It* (Grand Rapids MI: Eerdmans, 1993) 26.

5. Christina Rossetti, thinkexist.com/quotations/Rossetti.

6. John Claypool, *Tracks of a Fellow Struggler* (Waco TX: Word Books, 1974) 82.

7. Robert Emmons and Michael McCullough, "Counting Blessings Versus Burdens: An Experimental Investigation of Gratitude and Subjective Well-Being in Life," *Journal of Personality and Social Psychology* 84/2 (2003): 377–89.

8. Eugene Peterson, *A Long Obedience in the Same Direction* (Downers Grove IL: InterVarsity Press, 1980) 149–50.

9. Barbara Brown Taylor, *Leaving Church* (San Francisco: HarperSanFrancisco, 2006) 111.

# CHAPTER 3

# A Nation of Salesmen

## *(Do I Have to Sell Jesus?)*

To the simple, straightforward question, "Do I have to sell Jesus?" there is a simple, straightforward answer: *No.*

But let me be more emphatic. Please don't try to sell Jesus, because Jesus is not a commodity to be sold. He is not an automobile, vacuum cleaner, or insurance policy and shouldn't be treated as one. Jesus is a person, a mystery, and a wonder, but he is most assuredly not a commodity that can be sold to another person.

If we try to sell Jesus, we cheapen him. We make him into the best and latest product without which our family and friends cannot be happy or successful or "saved." In essence, we turn Jesus into a product that could be advertised on one of those TV infomercials. But discerning people will be repulsed by our efforts to sell Jesus and might, in fact, be forever turned off to the gospel. If they see and hear Jesus pitched enough in the marketplace, they will write him off as just another gimmick they don't need.

So, no, we don't have to sell Jesus. But if we are serious about being his disciples, and if we are serious about following the mandates of Scripture, we do have to bear witness for him in the world. We do have to mediate the grace and goodness of Christ to others. We do have to be "salt" and "light," as Jesus commanded in the Sermon on the Mount. But selling Jesus in the marketplace? Never.

I say that emphatically because I spent the first thirty years of my life trying to sell Jesus. That was what I learned evangelism was. It was selling Jesus to others. I attended classes, read books, and heard sermons on evangelism that, in effect, encouraged me to become a salesman for Jesus. I learned how to manipulate any conversation toward "spiritual things," how to ask leading questions, how to present the "Roman Road" and the "Four Spiritual Laws," and how to close the deal by getting people to pray "the sinner's prayer."

I grew up believing that evangelism was selling Jesus and that the best evangelists were extroverts who would venture where angels feared to tread. Evangelists talked to people about Jesus on airplanes. They engaged strangers in conversation and got them converted on the spot. They never worried about what people thought of them; they were so consumed with passion and love for Christ that they would go anywhere and confront anyone with the gospel.

But then there was me. Shy. Never talking to people on airplanes. Never engaging strangers in conversation. Always worried about what people would think of me and never wanting to be a nuisance. There was me—the introvert, trying desperately to be an extrovert so that I could sell Jesus in the marketplace.

In the course of my life, I have not only attended evangelism seminars and read evangelism books. I have also worn "witnessing buttons," knocked on stranger's doors and handed out gospel tracts, invited friends to revivals at my church, and led my church in an "evangelism explosion." I have tried my best to sell Jesus.

But it didn't work for me, and I think it didn't work for two reasons.

First, I just could not be the extrovert demanded by that approach to evangelism. I am no salesman and would be just as inept selling cars, vacuum cleaners, and insurance policies as I was at selling Jesus. If evangelism is for bold people who will go where angels fear to tread and initiate relationships with strangers, then I am in big trouble. Talk about David trying to wear Saul's armor!

Second, selling Jesus didn't work because people in our day don't want to be sold anything. A writer named Earl Shorris wrote a book years ago titled *A Nation of Salesmen*. He said that America has become just that—a nation of salesmen, where everyone is hawking something. He also said that, in such a culture, people eventually become turned off to salesmanship of any kind. When you've been accosted by salesmen all day—at work, on television and radio, in the newspapers, on billboards, etc.—you're not particularly thrilled when someone knocks on your door wanting to sell you Jesus.

So I failed as an evangelist. I was too timid and the world was too leery, and what feeble evangelistic encounters I attempted ended in disaster. I was embarrassed. My prospective converts were embarrassed. And not one person was added to the kingdom of God because of my efforts.

Only later did I realize that the problem was not so much with me but with the definition of evangelism I had learned. Gradually, over the years, I realized that evangelism is not selling Jesus to people and that evangelism is not just for gregarious people who never met a stranger. I learned that evangelism is "being" something, not just "doing" something.

As I think back on it now, I had learned that evangelism is doing certain things—knowing techniques, asking questions, quoting Scriptures, and leading people in a prescribed prayer. The certain things an evangelist had to do were best accomplished by those extroverted people who could also succeed at selling cars, vacuum cleaners, and insurance policies. Evangelism was basically learning to use certain strategies to get people to say "yes" to Jesus.

But that approach to evangelism, as sincere as it is, is destined to fail for the two reasons I just mentioned. It excludes too many people—namely, all of us introverts who don't want to sell anyone anything. And it turns off most of the people in our society who are already sick to death of salesmanship. Suffice it to say that in our culture, the word "evangelism" does not have positive connotations to most people. If evangelism is selling Jesus, then I'm afraid evangelism is in for some hard times.

Let's get a new concept of evangelism. Let's think of evangelism not as selling Jesus to people but as *being* Jesus to people. Let's shift the focus from *doing* to *being*. In the process, I think we will discover that evangelism is something even we introverts can do and something even sales-weary consumers might respond to.

## Be Centered

When Jesus beckons us in the Sermon on the Mount to be "the salt of the earth" and "the light of the world," he is implying something we shouldn't miss. He is implying that we have to *be* something to represent him in the world.

Salt and light are not worried about techniques for becoming saltier and lighter; they just have to remain true to their nature. Salt has to be itself, full of pungent flavor, and it will affect everything it touches. Light has to be itself, too, full of illumination, and it will dispel darkness wherever it goes.

If salt and light will be true to their nature, they will naturally do their work and influence everything they come in contact with. The danger, as Jesus points out, is that salt can lose its savor, and light can be hidden under a bushel basket. But if salt and light will just do their natural work, they will affect their surroundings.

Anne Lamott has a great line in her book on writing, *Bird by Bird*: "Lighthouses don't go running all over an island looking for boats to save; they just stand there shining."[1] If we will stay centered on God, we will be lighthouses who just stand there shining.

"Centered precisely on what?" you might ask. I think the four things I focused on in the previous chapter would be a good place to start.

*We keep our lives focused on grace.* We receive the grace of God and let it do its work in our lives. That means we know that we are forgiven and free and can live like it.

*We keep our lives focused on faith.* We keep trusting in the grace of God, and we keep trying to be gracious and useful in our relationships. Grace is God's gift to us; faith is our gift to God. We receive God's grace and live for God in the world.

*We keep our lives focused on gratitude.* We constantly fend off resentment and regret by being grateful. We choose daily to say with the Apostle Paul, "I have learned to be content with whatever I have" (Phil 4:11b).

*And we keep our lives focused on humility.* We know that we have plenty to be humble about, so we honestly admit our flaws. And we know, too, that we will never serve other people as long as we are "above" them. Only humility—getting beneath others—will allow us to serve.

If we can keep our lives tethered to those four realities—grace, faith, gratitude, and humility—we stand a decent chance of being salt and light. If we lose any of those realities, our salt will lose its flavor, and our light will be placed under a bushel basket. We will stand there, as lighthouses do, but we will not shine.

How do we keep our attention riveted on those four things? How do we keep our lives, in other words, centered on God? I think the answer to those questions varies from person to person, but I can think of several tools that help me stay connected to God and the things that matter:

• Church—Being a vital part of a local church enables us to worship and study regularly, gives us a place to give and serve, and provides us community and fellowship. A vital, vibrant church can keep us focused on God and the spiritual dimension of life. I will have more to say on the thorny issue of church in a coming chapter.
• Scripture—Regular Bible study, both in a group and as individuals, can keep us aware of God and what God is saying to us. Scripture continues to be "a lamp unto our feet and a light unto our path" (Ps 119:105). We will examine ways to make the Bible more meaningful in a coming chapter, too.
• Prayer—Daily prayer keeps us talking and listening to God. Prayer is the vehicle by which we keep our communication current with God. As we pray without ceasing, we stay aware of God's presence in our lives and in our world. And we have a vehicle by which we can express our gratitude to God.
• Giving—When Jesus said, "For where your treasure is, there your heart will be also" (Matt 6:22), he was telling us something important. If we follow the trail of our expenditures, we will find our hearts—those things we value most. As we give to help others, we change our hearts and become more centered on God.
• Books—Both fiction and nonfiction can help us remember the things that matter. When I think about my own spiritual growth,

where would I be without Robert Capon, Frederick Buechner, Fred Craddock, Barbara Brown Taylor, Wendell Berry, Karl Olsson, and a host of other writers? Good books challenge us, keep us thinking, and nudge us toward truth.

• Serving—There is something about one act of kindness to one other person that clarifies our calling and encourages us to do another act of kindness. And that one act of kindness to one other person brings God into focus and reminds us that those who have received grace always bestow grace.

• Fasting—This can involve more than just not eating food. Fasting can enable us to get rid of a bunch of modern addictions so that we can return our focus to God. We can choose to fast from noise, television, the computer, the cell phone, work, spending, or any number of other things that consume us and keep us from seeking first the kingdom of God.

• Silence—Every day we could guard some time and spend it in silence. We could focus our attention on God and on the four things that should define us—grace, faith, gratitude, and humility. If nothing else, a time of silence each day would give us the opportunity to escape the frenzied pace of modern life and re-center our lives on God.

If we could use these tools—and perhaps others that would keep us from wandering away from God—we might actually succeed in becoming salt and light. We might become so peculiar, counter-cultural, joyful, and God-focused that we could go to the office, classroom, or ball field and just stand there, shining.

The place to begin in any approach to evangelism, it seems to me, is right here. We change. We become different. We get a whole new set of priorities. And then we live naturally and freely as "the salt of the earth" and "the light of the world."

## Be Present

In her book *The Total Image*, Virginia Stem Owens writes,

> We do not hand our children a book on how to behave when once they learn to read. We know the terrifying truth that they must

learn from living with us, watching us. The means of conveying the information needed to become a human being is necessarily communal. Infants incapable of speech learn their most fundamental and essential information about the universe from the early, inarticulate years. To "know" a person means, if nothing else, to have been in that one's presence, to hear the voice, to see the face.[2]

That, I think, is a fundamental tenet of evangelism. Evangelists are present. They know people, care for people, have a relationship with people. Our family and friends don't get to know God because we pass along profound pieces of theological information to them. They get to know God because they know *us*. They've been in our presence, heard our voices, and seen our faces.

What that means, in a practical way, is that we strive to know and love a few people deeply. We don't have to distribute gospel tracts to strangers to be effective evangelists; we just have to be present to a few people who are in our lives. We go to their birthday parties. We watch them play softball. We drink coffee with them at the coffee shop. We laugh when they laugh and cry when they cry. And, in the process, we get to be salt and light to them. Even if we never quote the Bible to them or say a prayer with them, we are the presence of Christ to them.

Owens continues,

> It is a very simple and obvious proposition I make: a person whether human or divine, cannot be known—as a person rather than an image—except by immediate presence. If we want to project an image, either of Christians or the church, we can do that by means of television, magazines, books, billboards, movies, bumper stickers, buttons, records, and posters. If we want people to know Christ, we must be there face to face, bearing Christ within us.[3]

You'll remember that when asked to name the greatest commandment in the law, Jesus said that we are to love God with all of our minds, hearts, souls, and strength, and we are to love our neighbors as we love ourselves. In essence, the greatest commandment is to love God and people.

The first two qualities of an effective evangelist I've mentioned follow that great commandment. We begin by centering our lives on God and embodying grace, faith, gratitude, and humility. Then we become present to the people we love. We are with them, literally and spiritually, bearing their burdens and trying to be salt and light to them.

In the process of loving God and loving people, the best evangelism happens. Naturally and without pressure, we mediate the presence and love of Christ to the people we know and love.

## Be Real

At least in the best of all worlds, that's the way it is *supposed* to work. In actuality, sometimes the way we connect to people is not altogether winsome and persuasive. In actuality, sometimes the people in our lives look at us and our faith and are not evangelized at all.

Sometimes, they see us as fake, "plastic" saints, quoting our Bible verses and attending our Sunday school classes. They see us as naïve religionists, clueless when it comes to the negative stuff they are dealing with—lust, doubt, anger, and confusion, just to mention a few.

The best, most effective Christian evangelists, therefore, will be real people, fully acquainted with lust, doubt, anger, and confusion and not ashamed to admit it. They will not be ivory-tower saints, lobbing advice from afar, but flesh-and-blood strugglers conversant with life in the trenches. And in the trenches, they will be people of grace, faith, gratitude, and humility, and they will be salt and light in the process.

In his book *Orbiting the Giant Hairball (A Corporate Fool's Guide to Surviving with Grace)*, Gordon MacKenzie writes of the artificiality that creeps into most businesses and corporations:

> How do we become so bogus? Well, our artificiality is caused, in part, by the many teachers and trainers who work so hard to instill a professionalism that prizes correctness over authenticity and originality. Flesh-and-blood students persevere the rigors of broadcast school only to emerge with voices as unreal as their pancake make-up. Budding designers, capable of passion, sweat the grind in

schools of architecture and graduate to create environments uncon-
nected to the lusciousness of life. Diamonds-in-the-rough enter
business schools and come out the other end as so many polished
clones addicted to the dehumanizing power of classification and
systematization.[4]

Those of us in the church could add our own addendum to that para-
graph: our artificiality is caused, in part, by parents, preachers, and
professors who have convinced us that the best Christian witnesses
are those who are above reproach, never question or doubt, and never,
ever stumble into sin.

In short, we have been taught to believe that the best evangelists
are people who look down on sinners and then try to pull them out
of the quagmires of sin they have created. But certainly the evangelists
themselves have never been in any of those quagmires. Certainly the
evangelists themselves are not acquainted with lust, doubt, anger, and
confusion. In essence, certainly the evangelists themselves are not real
people.

But we must be. If we are going to bear witness for Christ in the
real world, we must be real people. As we stay centered on God and
are present to the people around us, we also live with authenticity.
We hurt. We doubt. We get angry. But through it all, we trust the
One who was betrayed, whipped, and crucified, the One who
endured the worst the world could toss at him and came out victori-
ous on the other side.

It would be wonderful if Jesus' followers could be as real as
he was.

## Be Quiet

One of the problems with the concept of evangelism I grew up with
is that I, as the evangelist, was always in control. In effect, I was a
salesman making my pitch to an unconverted sinner. But I had to be
in control. I had to initiate the conversation. And, even if I asked
some leading questions, the point was to put me back in control so
I could close the deal.

The assumption was that I had the answers and my "prospect" didn't. I was saved and my prospect was lost. I knew the Bible and my prospect didn't. And I had experienced God, while my prospect had not.

When you think about it, that approach seems terribly arrogant. This was not intended to be a conversation; it was designed to be a sales pitch. I was to be the talker, and my poor prospect was to be the listener. And I was going to be so persuasive and biblical that my prospect would finally see the error of his ways and come to Christ.

But was it possible that my prospects weren't ignorant after all? Was it possible that they had had some experiences of their own with God? Was it possible that they had a faith tradition of their own? Was it possible, heaven forbid, that they had some things to teach me if only I had actually engaged them in conversation and listened to what they had to say?

There was no room for listening or silence or learning in that approach to evangelism. It was a one-way assault of propositions and Bible verses, and, as I said, it was destined to fail, destined even to make some of its victims see "evangelism" as a dirty word.

Good evangelists know how to be quiet, how to respect the privacy of others, how to listen to the hopes and hurts of people, and how to be silent enough not to interfere with what God might be doing in a person's life.

The old approach focused on talking; this new approach focuses on listening. The old approach was about noise; the new approach is about quiet.

Hear novelist Walker Percy:

> . . . in these times everyone is an apostle of sorts, ringing doorbells and bidding his neighbor to believe this and do that. In such times, when everyone is saying "Come!" and when radio and television say nothing but "Come!" it may be that the best way to say "Come" is to remain silent. Sometimes silence itself is a "Come!"[5]

For sure, sometimes silence is a statement of respect, a way of recognizing another's opinions and pondering another's experience with

God. The new evangelism that might reach people in our culture will have to be a quiet kind of evangelism practiced by Christians who are not afraid to be silent and listen.

## Evangelism and the Golden Rule

I can almost assure you that some time in the next month or so there will be a knock on our front door. I will look out the peephole and see that our visitors are nicely dressed, have religious tracts in their hands, and would like me to open the door so that they can engage me in conversation and give me some of their literature. I'm sure they are sincere, dedicated people. But I will look out that peephole and go back to watching television or reading my book. I will not be in the mood to be evangelized. I'm guessing most of my neighbors feel the same way.

Before we launch any kind of evangelism, it would be wise to consider the Golden Rule and do to others what we would have them do to us. If someone was intent on evangelizing us, how would we like that to be done? Do we want strangers knocking on our door? Do we want acquaintances explaining tracts to us? Do we want a preacher explaining Bible verses to us? If a Jew, Buddhist, Muslim, or Mormon wanted to evangelize us, how would we like that done?

Well, honestly, most of us would say we don't want it done at all. We know what we believe, are grateful for our relationship with God, and would feel offended if someone suggested our way was invalid or misguided. For most of us, even we long-time Christians, "evangelism" is not a compelling word.

Evangelism might be something we feel we should do, but it is most assuredly not something we want done to us. So let's apply the Golden Rule and consider how we would like to be evangelized before we attempt to evangelize others.

What if we went back to the drawing board and came up with a new idea about evangelism?

What if evangelism had nothing to do with selling Jesus or persuading people who really don't want to be persuaded?

What if evangelism was simply about being genuinely centered on, and connected, to God?

What if tending to our own relationship with God, not others' relationship with God, was the first priority of evangelism? What if becoming salt and light was more important than knowing sales techniques?

What if evangelism was about being connected to people, so that we know them and they know us, and we don't have to cram our faith down their throats? What if we're so present to people that they just catch grace and faith from being around us?

What if evangelism was about being a genuine human being, not a "plastic" saint? What if we were free to express our doubts, struggle with our sins, and admit our humanity? Would that ruin our witness to the world, or would it just make us more credible? Would it finally free us to be real instead of religious?

And what if evangelism was about being quiet? What if we trusted that God was already working in people's lives and that we might best help that process by listening? What if we so respected people and the Holy Spirit that we didn't mess things up by talking too much? What if we saw our role as quietly enabling the Spirit to keep working in a person's life?

If we began to see evangelism this way, I think two things could happen. First, I think many of us who decided long ago that we didn't have the "gift of evangelism" would reconsider. If evangelism is being centered, present, real, and quiet, we might be suited for the job after all. This new concept of evangelism would open up possibilities for us "quiet Christians" that we've never seen before. We could be our introverted selves and still do evangelism.

Second, I think that many people who have been turned off to evangelism and put off by pushy Christians would find this approach attractive. For a change, they would feel like Christians respected and listened to them. For a change, they would not feel "talked down to" by their evangelical friends. And, for a change, they just might have ears to hear the good news of the gospel.

In *The Total Image*, Virginia Owens says,

Christians speak earnestly about "meeting individual needs." Then they try to do it by techniques. Any technique, by its very nature, cannot meet *individual* needs, which are, by definition, unique. The whole point of technique is to meet mass needs. . . . But one of the amazing things about the gospels is the absence of technique in Jesus' ministry. There are an extraordinary number of intimate conversations with Jesus recorded and each one is unique. He had different answers for each seeker. Some he commanded to follow; others he told to go home. Never once did he distribute tracts containing either spiritual laws or plans of salvation.[6]

So what did Jesus do? He loved God with all of his heart, mind, soul, and strength. He loved people and served them in tangible, costly ways. He was a real human being who told stories, cried in anguish, experienced the rejection of his friends, and died a cruel and unjustified death. And he quietly trusted that God was at work in the world and in the lives of the people he knew. In short, he was centered, present, real, and quiet.

Here's hoping Jesus can be a model for all Christians, but especially for those of us who gave up on evangelism a long time ago.

## For Reflection or Discussion

1. Have you ever felt pressure to "sell Jesus"? How have you dealt with that pressure?

2. Have you ever known a person who had a natural, relaxed approach to evangelism that led people to faith in God? What attributes did that person have?

3. Do you think we need a new definition of "evangelism"? How would you define or describe this new evangelism?

4. What do you do to keep your life centered in God?

5. Do you make it a priority to be present to the people you know and love? How?

6. Do most Christians seem real or fake (or something in-between)?

7. Do you agree that we Christians need to listen more and talk less? Why or why not?

8. What, if anything, can we do to rescue "evangelism" and make it a good word again?

## NOTES

1. Anne Lamott, *Bird by Bird* (New York: Doubleday, 1994) 236.

2. Virginia Stem Owens, *The Total Image* (Grand Rapids MI: Eerdmans, 1980) 80.

3. Ibid., 81.

4. Gordon MacKenzie, *Orbiting the Giant Hairball* (New York: Viking, 1996) 130.

5. Walker Percy, *The Message in the Bottle* (New York: Farrar, Strauss, & Giroux, 1975) 148.

6. Owens, *The Total Image*, 79–80.

# Some Said It Thundered

*(Does God Ever Say Anything?)*

An interesting though little-known passage in John's Gospel gets to the heart of a dilemma most of us eventually encounter in our relationship with God. In the passage, Jesus is facing death and tells his followers about his struggle.

> "Now my soul is troubled. And what should I say—'Father, save me from this hour?' No, it is for this reason that I have come to this hour. Father, glorify your name."
>
> Then a voice came from heaven, "I have glorified it and will glorify it again."
>
> The crowd standing there heard it and said that it was thunder.
>
> Others said, "An angel has spoken to him." (John 12:27-29)

So which was it—God or thunder? Was the sound they heard the voice of an angel of God, or was that simply the rumbling of thunder in the distance? Those who had that experience that day left with different interpretations of what had happened. Some said they heard the voice of God, but some said it thundered.

Poll the American populace on the question, "Does God ever say anything?" and I suspect you will get similar results. Some will say that God does speak and that we humans had better be listening, and others will scoff at the idea of a talkative deity. In our day, as in the first century, some say it is the voice of God, while others swear it is thunder.

I have to admit that I have always been skeptical of people claiming to have heard the voice of God. When I was a pastor, people would occasionally come to my study to tell me about a word they had received from the Lord. "God told me to . . . ," they would say. Or, "The Lord spoke very clearly to me and said . . . ." Inevitably I was wary of their story. I have never been that sure of God's voice and don't trust those who are.

And yet . . . in the Bible God often speaks to people in clear, unmistakable ways, and they hear and respond to the word of the Lord. It happened to Abram, Noah, Moses, and Saul of Tarsus, so who am I to declare that God can't speak to people? Who am I to scoff at those who claim to have heard the voice of God?

In his book *The Disappearance of God*, Richard Friedman traces an intriguing phenomenon in Scripture. As a Jewish scholar, he deals only with the Old Testament, but he traces how God gradually withdraws as the story unfolds. At the beginning of the Old Testament, God speaks, sends fire and flood, and frequently performs miracles. God is a hands-on deity, and people experience God face to face and person to person.

But that changes as the story develops. By the end of the Old Testament, God has withdrawn and speaks primarily through the prophets and a few chosen spokesmen. People experience God indirectly. The presence of God is a mediated presence. The Old Testament, Friedman contends, is the story of the disappearance of God.

Though Friedman doesn't deal with the New Testament in his book, the same phenomenon happens there, too. At the beginning of the New Testament story, Jesus confronts people directly, reveals God directly, and performs miracles directly. But, by the end of the New Testament, Jesus has ascended into heaven, and people experience God indirectly—through the church, letters from church leaders, and the enigmatic Holy Spirit. Like the Old Testament, the New Testament is the story of the disappearance of God. (See Richard Friedman,

*The Disappearance of God* [New York: Little, Brown, and Company, 1995].)

Whether you buy that theory or not, most of us would have to admit that God has disappeared from our own experience. At least, God has disappeared from our experience if we measure revelation by *direct* manifestations—a voice, fire and wind from on high, miracles, or other obvious evidence of God's presence.

If, or when, we experience God, most of us experience God *indirectly*—through Scripture, the church, nature, music, or other people. In truth, we're not exactly sure if it is God that we're experiencing, but we believe it to be so and even make some major decisions based on these indirect manifestations of God. We are guided by what we take to be divine hints and supernatural hunches.

The dilemma we face is how to know if these hints and hunches are indeed the voice of God. Is this God speaking to us, or is it circumstance? Is this divine intervention in our lives, or just the playing of old religious tapes from childhood? In essence, we're still back there in John 12: Is this God . . . or thunder?

When we wrestle with those questions, what we really want to know, of course, is, *Does God ever say anything to me personally?* We're not so concerned about what God might say to others or how God might make himself known in history. We're concerned about hearing the voice of God in our own lives. We want to make sure that if God does say a word, we hear it. We want to know the will of God, the voice of God, *for us.*

## Is that You, God?

The problem is that God doesn't seem to be saying much. Or if God *is* saying something to us, we're not particularly adept at hearing it. Robert Capon, in his book *Hunting the Divine Fox*, writes,

> Everyone agrees, of course, that what we need most is To Do the Will of God. The trouble is that very few people, unless they are faking it, know what the will of God for them is. There is a lot of pious talk about finding out about whether it is the will of God for you to marry Irving, or become a priest, or take the veil; but in all

honesty, what you are really going to do is what *your* will on the subject is, and whether you have enough nerve to go through with it. A few special types with inside tracks may get their answers straight from God, but the rest of us get them from ourselves—and from Irving, the Bishop, and the Reverend Mother, respectively. God is notoriously silent; and when he speaks, it is usually in parables, just so no one will be able to claim too much clarity and insight. He runs the world, not only with his hands in his pockets, but with his mouth mostly shut.[1]

That, most assuredly, is not the kind of God we want, but truth demands us to admit that it *is* the kind of God we have. We want a God who not only speaks but who speaks loudly and clearly. When it comes to something as important as the will of God for our lives, we want God to be both audible and explicit.

For years, I assumed the will of God would be (1) clearly communicated to me and (2) spelled out in minute detail. I assumed that God would make it plain where I was supposed to go to college, what my major should be, which young woman I was supposed to marry, where we were supposed to live, how many children we should have, and what vocation I was supposed to pursue. All of that, I assumed, would be spelled out in exact detail so that I could know and live the will of God.

I would later learn that I was wrong on both counts. God would not speak very plainly, and the details of God's will would unfold in what seemed to be a haphazard jumble of coincidence and circumstance. Discerning the will of God felt precariously like flying by the seat on my own pants.

But I did discover, years ago, two statements from two of my favorite authors that helped me as I tried to find and live the will of God. One was from Robert Capon in the book I just quoted, *Hunting the Divine Fox*. In that book, Capon says, "The will of God is not a list of stops for us to make to pick up mouthwash, razor blades, and a pound of chopped chuck on the way home. It is his longing that we will take the risk of being nothing but ourselves, desperately in love."[2]

The other statement was from Frederick Buechner in his book *Wishful Thinking*: "The place where God calls you is the place where your deep gladness and the world's deep hunger meet."[3]

From those two statements, I was able to cobble together a concept of the will of God that made sense to me at the time and still makes sense to me more than thirty years later. The concept of the will of God I got from Capon and Buechner has enabled me to navigate through some treacherous waters, and I have come to depend on it as a reliable guide.

From their two statements about the will of God, I extracted four questions that I have asked myself whenever I stood at one of those crucial crossroads in my life. In lieu of voices from heaven and blinding lights, which I would have preferred, these questions have helped me, I think, discern God's will.

**Does This Make Me *Me*?**

After telling us that the will of God is not making a bunch of stops on the way home to pick up mouthwash, razor blades, and a pound of chopped chuck—not, in other words, spelled out in minute detail—Capon says that it is God's longing "that we take the risk of being nothing but ourselves . . . ."

The first question, then, is, "*Does this make me* me*?*" In other words, will this job, this person, this move, this church, or whatever I'm trying to decide enable me to be my authentic self? Is it in line with my personality and temperament? Will this decision line up with who I am so that I have some of those glorious moments where I can say, "For this I was made?"

I had many of those moments when I was a pastor. Though there were times when I felt like an introvert in an extrovert's job, there were other times when I felt like I was exactly where I was supposed to be. I remember thinking on several occasions, usually while I was preaching on Sunday morning, that this was precisely what I was supposed to be doing. It just felt right, and I knew I was squarely in the center of God's will.

I mentioned in the first chapter of this book that when we live only by expert advice, we abandon our lives and forsake our uniqueness. Each of us is a unique creation of God, and I'm suggesting here that a part of God's will for each of us is finding jobs, people, and circumstances that will enable us to be who we are.

If the job is not *you*, don't take it. If the prospective spouse will not let you be *you*, call off the wedding. If the church will not let you be *you*, move your membership. A vital part of the will of God for each of us is being true to the difference to which we have been created and called.

Sadly, it often takes a lifetime of living to learn this. As we get older, we start to realize that the instructional manual we were handed when we were young and told to build our lives by is, in fact, not going to build anything even resembling who we really are. If we follow that manual, we will end up on our deathbeds filled with sadness and regret. Why did we keep doing those things? Why did we forsake our real loves and inclinations to follow that manual's silly advice? Why didn't we have the courage to be ourselves?

If there is any advantage to growing older, it might be right at this point. Older people know that the manual doesn't work. Older people know that they have precious little time left to be themselves, so they're willing to risk it and give it a go.

Anna Quindlen, in her book *Lots of Candles, Plenty of Cake*, writes,

> One of the greatest glories of growing older is the willingness to ask why and, getting no good answer, deciding to follow my own inclinations and desires. Asking why is the way to wisdom. Why are we supposed to want possessions we don't need and work that seems besides the point and tight shoes and a fake tan? Why are we supposed to turn our backs on those who have preceded us and to snipe at those who come after? When we were small children we asked "Why?" constantly. Asking the question now is more a matter of testing the limits of what sometimes seems a narrow world. One of the useful things about age is realizing conventional wisdom is often simply inertia with a candy coating of conformity.[4]

That last line is worth committing to memory: "Conventional wisdom is often simply inertia with a candy coating of conformity."

That's why many older people thumb their noses at conventional wisdom. They have learned that it's okay to be different. No, that it's *mandatory* to be different.

That old guy in the one-piece jumpsuit and the ball cap and the tennis shoes? The guy you scoff at as old-fashioned and out of style? The guy you hope you will never turn into? Don't be so quick to judge that old guy. He's wise enough not to care about fashion. He's wise enough not to worship the instruction manual. He's even wise enough not to care what you think about him.

He has moved beyond conventional wisdom and is content to be who he is—jumpsuit and all. That old guy, as out of touch with the real world as he seems to be, may be closer to the will of God than you are. At least he's willing to be himself.

He, at least, knows that each of us needs to get on with the business of being nothing but ourselves. The marathoner doesn't have to play linebacker. The stand-up comic doesn't have to work in a cubicle. And the woman who loves to stay home with her kids doesn't have to have a career in the business world.

We're all free to be ourselves, and whatever or whoever enables us to do that is leading us to the will of God.

### Does This Make Me Love?

The will of God, Capon says, is God's longing that we will take the risk of being nothing but ourselves, *desperately in love*. The second question we can ask when considering any decision, then, is *"Does this make me love?"* Will this job, spouse, church, or decision lead me to love and enable me to love?

I have long been grateful for that unnamed lawyer who came to Jesus inquiring about the greatest commandment in the law. Some scholars think it might have been a trick question, designed to back Jesus into a corner. After all, who in his right mind would try to pick out one supreme commandment out of the more than six hundred commandments in the Old Testament? But whether it was a trick question or not, the lawyer's question gave Jesus the opportunity to condense all of those more than six hundred commandments down to their essence. "He said to him, 'You shall love the Lord your God with all your heart, and with all your soul, and with all your mind. This is the greatest and first commandment. And the second is like it: You shall love your neighbor as yourself. On those two commandments hang all the law and prophets'" (Matt 22:37-40).

Boil those words down even further, and the commandments are about two things: loving God and loving people. That's the essence of all the Old Testament commandments and the essence of a life with God. It is God's will that we love God and our neighbor.

The problem with that, of course, is that it is about as exciting as reading the classified section of the newspaper. Announce from the pulpit one Sunday that the Bible is primarily about loving God and loving people, and you will get a hearty "Amen" from the deacon on the back row. Then he will nod back to sleep and half the congregation will nod with him. Telling people to love God and one another might be true, but it has a "wow factor" of zero. Everybody knows it, but nobody wants to hear it again.

But since Jesus did say it, and since we have taken a vow to treat his word with utmost respect, we should try to shake off our lethargy and think about what he said. The essence of the commandments is love. We are to love God, and we are to love people. Since those two things capture the essence of the commandments, they also define the will of God for us. It is God's will that we love God and love our neighbor.

That means, first, that we can't forget the spiritual, transcendent dimension of life. We are to focus on loving God. We can't get so caught up in raising a family, making money, becoming a success, winning on the PGA tour, or looking like a young beauty queen that we forget God. Whatever it takes—wearing phylacteries, attending church every Sunday, having a personal devotional time every morning, saying a prayer before every meal, or spending time each evening counting our blessings—that is what we will do to remember God and to stoke our love for God.

If there is a God, if that God is full of love and grace, if that God gave us Jesus to reconcile us to himself, and if we now live as free and forgiven people in the world, how can we keep from singing? How can we keep from loving God? How can we keep from obeying the great commandment?

Then there is the second commandment that is like it—loving our neighbor as we love ourselves. Of the two, that one might be the hardest to obey. Frankly, people can be a colossal pain. Loving a sinless, gracious God is easier than loving sinful, selfish people.

But there is one thing in Jesus' statement that gives us hope. We are to love *our neighbor*, he says. That command is singular, focused, and personal. God might be big enough to love the whole world, but Jesus says we are to love our neighbor. That seems to at least imply that if we can love a few people with a concentrated love, we have kept this commandment and settled into the will of God.

So, when we come to those crossroads in our lives when we have to make a crucial decision, this is another factor to add to the mix: Will this job enable me to love God and people? Will this person enable me to love God and people? Will this move enable me to be more loving, more focused on God and the people who matter most to me?

We are to take the risk of being nothing but ourselves, *desperately in love*.

### Does This Make Me Glad?

Frederick Buechner's statement in *Wishful Thinking* gives us two more dimensions to consider as we try to discern the voice of God. When Buechner writes, "The place God calls you to is the place where your deep gladness and the world's deep hunger meet," he points us toward our own gladness and the world's need.

The intersection of those two realities, he suggests, puts us in the center of God's will. So, in addition to *"Does this make me me?"* and *"Does this make me love?"* we can add a third question: *"Does this make me glad?"* Where is the place that gives me deep gladness, the person who most makes me glad, the work that fills me with joy? If I can find the center of my joy, I have taken a big step toward discovering God's will.

I hate to admit it, but I spent a good portion of my life believing just the opposite was true. I grew up believing that whatever I didn't want to do was probably the very thing God was calling me to do. My concept of God was so negative that I thought God couldn't possibly want me to be happy.

Since I didn't want to leave my family and become a missionary in Africa, that's probably what God wanted me to do. Since I couldn't bear the thought of being an evangelist and selling Jesus to my friends, that's probably what God was asking me to do. Since I really wanted to get married and have children, God probably wanted me to be single and celibate. I grew up with the notion that my will and God's will would always be at cross purposes.

It was a great relief to finally get to the place in my life where I had a God who wanted me to be happy. Instead of assuming that God's will was for me to be miserable and faithful, I started thinking that those two things were not mutually exclusive. I could actually be happy and faithful, and, in fact, the intersection of those two realities was precisely where God wanted me to be.

What makes us glad? What do we love to do? What do we look forward to doing? I am writing these words to you on my laptop while sipping a cup of coffee at Starbucks. My wife stopped by a moment ago to say hello, and I said to her, "I'm pretty sure we have found the good life." We gave each other a quiet "high five."

This, for me, is the good life. Others would probably find it boring and tedious. But I love to write. I love to be alone. I love to sip coffee. I love to theologize. And I'm getting to do all of those things right here at Starbucks. Dare I say that I have found the will of God for my life?

Several months ago, I was invited to preach at a fine church in the Washington, DC, area. The church had a casual service in the fellowship hall on Saturday night and three services on Sunday morning. I was scheduled to preach in all four of those services.

I preached Saturday evening, then got up early on Sunday to preach at the contemplative service at 8:15, the contemporary service at 9:30, and the classic service at 11:00. By the time I was finished with the fourth service, I was one tired preacher.

I asked the pastor of the church how he did that week after week. His answer was, "I love to preach, and, as an extrovert, the four services really excite me. By the end of the fourth service, I'm really 'wired.' Preaching four times doesn't tire me out; it fires me up."

As an introvert, I was not "wired" at the end of those four services. I was drained and sorely in need of a nap! But the pastor, an extrovert who thrived on activity and people, was energized by those services. They filled him with gladness, and I thought as I flew home from that trip that he is exactly where he needs to be. The will of God for him is to be preaching four services every weekend. The will of God for me was to be on that airplane headed back to my world of Starbucks, writing, and solitude.

In a "Peanuts" comic strip years ago, the inimitable theologian Charlie Brown said, "Joy is the most infallible proof of the presence of God." As usual, Charlie is right. Joy is the most infallible proof of the presence of God in our life and also the most infallible proof that we are living squarely in the middle of God's will.

### Does This Make Me Useful?

Buechner said the place God calls us to is the place where our deep gladness and *the world's deep hunger meet.* That adds a fourth dimension for us to consider as we think about God's will: *"Does this make me useful?"* Where can we go and what can we do to address the world's deep hunger?

The first three questions were focused inside us and beckoned us to look inward and determine what makes us authentically ourselves, what makes us love God and people, and what makes us glad. This fourth question beckons us to look outward and to consider how we can best make a difference in the world. How can we be ourselves, love God and others, find great joy in what we do, *and* influence our world?

The burning passion of Jesus' life was the kingdom of God. He came into the world to announce that kingdom, tell stories about that kingdom, and get people excited about that kingdom. When he bodily left this earth, he left behind a vision of this new kingdom. His followers caught the vision from him and determined to finish his work. In spite of opposition and even persecution, they were going to continue Jesus' work of building the kingdom of God.

It is, even now, the primary task of Jesus' followers. Those of us who have vowed to live for him have taken upon ourselves the task of building the kingdom of God right where we are. As we love our families, serve our church, do our jobs, coach our teams, cook our meals, and do all the other things normal people do, we do so with one overarching goal—to build a kingdom of grace, faith, gratitude, and humility where we are.

We might not be able to do everything, but we can do something. We can grab hold of the rope in front of us and, with God's help, pull with all of our might. If we can get enough people pulling on that rope, we just might succeed in establishing the kingdom of God in our home, church, neighborhood, office, school, or town. Even if we don't succeed, we have at least given our lives to the task Jesus thought was the most important task in the world.

So, as we consider the will of God for our lives, this is an essential component. How can I best build the kingdom of God? Will this job enable me to build the kingdom of God? Will attending this school prepare me to build the kingdom of God? Will this person be a partner in building the kingdom of God? What will enable me to put grace, love, gratitude, and humility into the world?

Yes, we want to be authentically ourselves. Yes, we want to love God and people. And yes, we want to be glad and have joy in our lives. But we also want to be useful. We want to link our lives with the passion of Jesus and make building the kingdom of God our life's task.

## Stumbling to Zion

There is, as you probably already know from your own experience, a fly in the ointment in this talk about the will of God. In his book *Understanding God's Will*, Kyle Lake writes,

> Some will say that seven steps to understanding God's will—if accurately considered and adhered to—goes as follows: Look to God for guidance through consistent prayer. Look to the Scriptures for direction. Seek the advice of upstanding God-followers in whom you trust. Find a sense of inner peace about the direction you are

facing. Okay, maybe that's just four. And actually, these questions are still imperative to ask. But what happens when the bottom falls out and it's not because you didn't pray? You *did* pray! You *did* look to solid people for guidance and wisdom and never once received the proverbial red flag! You *did* look to the Scriptures, and the Scriptures seemed to resonate with your decision as well. And not only that, but your soul oozed peace. If you ever felt confident about God's direction, this was it. It all seemed to add up at every turn. And then it didn't.[5]

Or, to use the four truths I've mentioned in this chapter:

• What if you have earnestly tried to make decisions in keeping with your truest self?
• What if you have done everything with an eye toward loving God and the people in your life?
• What if you have been diligent in seeking joy and doing things that make you glad?
• And what if you have tried your best to be useful and to join Christ in building the kingdom of God where you are?

What if you have done all the right things—and the bottom still fell out? The marriage collapsed. The job turned out to be a disaster. The move to a new town created unimaginable problems. The decision to retire led to boredom and depression.

You felt so sure when you made your decision, but time has proven you wrong. You made a wrong decision, misread the will of God, and seem to be stuck now in a quagmire of your own making.

Well, welcome to the real world! And welcome to the world of Christian discipleship, where most of us misread the will of God on a fairly regular basis. In truth, we Christians are not marching to Zion, the beautiful city of God; we're *stumbling* to Zion.

Our path is not a straightforward dash toward God's perfect will for our lives; it is a zigzagging, roundabout journey filled with road-blocks and detours. God doesn't shout, and most of us are not adept at picking up on quiet clues, so missing the will of God is a common phenomenon among Christians.

When I look back on my life, I realize that I found the will of God in a lot of areas. But when I retired as a pastor a couple of years ago to devote more time to writing, I entered into new territory. All of a sudden, I didn't have a job, a church, or a compelling reason to get out of bed in the morning. Old things passed away, and behold, all things became new. I had to start asking fresh questions for myself about the will of God.

How can I be my authentic self now that I'm no longer a pastor? How can I love God and people now that I'm no longer under the steeple? How can I find gladness in my new life? And how can I work to build the kingdom of God now that it's no longer my job?

This new era in my life has reminded me that finding the will of God is an ongoing, never-ending process. Life unfolds like a scroll, and so does the will of God. We never get to the point where we can gloat and smugly declare ourselves forever ensconced in God's will. I might have made some good decisions in the past, but today I have new decisions to make, and whether or not I find God's will is yet to be determined.

But at least I have those four clues. At least I can look for people, places, and activities that make me genuinely myself, that help me love God and others, that make me joyful, and that make me useful in building God's kingdom where I am.

Of course, I'm still hoping for that voice from heaven or that blinding light from on high. But, given my experience with God so far, I'm not holding my breath.

This I know, too: even if I get that voice from heaven, there will be someone somewhere who will say that it was only thunder.

## For Reflection or Discussion

1. Do you struggle to discern the difference between "God and thunder"? Has God ever spoken to you? How did you know it was God?

2. Are you suspicious when people say they've heard the voice of God? How do we justify our suspicions in light of the biblical passages about God speaking to people?

3. Have you ever thought about the disappearance of God in the Bible? Do you agree or disagree with that idea?

4. What situations or activities make you feel like "you"? When do you feel most yourself?

5. What situations or activities in your life enable you to love others in tangible ways?

6. When was the last time you felt "deep gladness"? How can you get back to that place?

7. Are you making a difference to anyone else? What are you doing to build the kingdom of God?

8. Have you ever misread the will of God? How did you recover from your mistake, and what did you learn from the experience?

## NOTES

1. Robert Farrar Capon, *Hunting the Divine Fox* (New York: Seabury Press, 1974) 39–40.

2. Ibid., 41.

3. Frederick Buechner, *Wishful Thinking* (New York: Harper & Row, 1973) 95.

4. Anna Quindlen, *Lots of Candles, Plenty of Cake* (New York: Random House, 2012) 42.

5. Kyle Lake, *Understanding God's Will* (Lake Mary FL: Relevant Books, 2005) xxvii.

# CHAPTER 5

# Welcome to McDonald's

*(Can I Survive the Church?)*

A clever title can put a book on the bestseller list.

In the 1970s a writer named Fritz Ridenour wrote a book titled *How to Be a Christian without Being Religious.* The book became a bestseller, and I'm guessing the title had a lot to do with that. Isn't that what we would all like—to be genuinely Christian without being stuffy and religious?

More recently, Diana Butler Bass has written a book titled *Christianity After Religion: The End of Church and the Birth of a New Spiritual Awakening.* I think that title has elicited a lot of interest as well. After all, who among us wouldn't like to move beyond legalistic religion to have a new spiritual awakening? Who among us wouldn't want to find a faith that goes beyond boring sermons and tired worship services? We would all like to find a Christianity *after* religion.

I can think of another book title that might capture the attention of a lot of modern readers: *How to Be a Christian without Going to Church.* I say that because more and more people are finding the church unattractive and opting to attend "Saint Mattress" on Sunday morning. A book suggesting that a person could be a legitimate Christian without having to attend church would probably find a large and receptive audience.

In *Christianity After Religion*, Diana Butler Bass writes,

> All sorts of people—even mature, faithful Christians—are finding
> conventional religion increasingly less satisfying, are attending
> church less regularly, and are longing for new expressions of spiritual
> community. As I traveled the country sharing my research with pas-
> tors, they began to relate on-the-ground stories that echoed the
> polling data. "People just don't come to church anymore," pastors
> told me. "It doesn't really matter what we do or how solid our com-
> munity is. Even those who consider themselves 'good' members
> only come once a month or so now."[1]

For decades, church attendance in Europe has been plummeting, but
we Americans assumed our faith was heartier than that of European
Christians. We assumed we would never see our churches empty, our
choirs singing and pastors preaching to unoccupied pews. But the
statistics show we're following the same path as the churches in
Europe. Every year, more and more Americans are deciding not to go
to church.

That reality becomes even more alarming when we see the statistics on church attendance for young adults. For whatever reason—
and many have been suggested—young adults are abandoning the
church at an unprecedented pace. Currently, some 25 to 30 percent
of adults under the age of thirty claim no religious affiliation at all,
and the number is climbing every year.

Several years ago, my two-year-old grandson, Bodie, went to
church on Easter Sunday with his parents. They nestled into a pew at
the back of the sanctuary, and all went well—for a while. But Bodie
grew increasingly restless and eventually announced in a loud voice,
"I'm done with church." And he was. His father had to take him outside and entertain him until the service was over.

Evidently, Bodie is not the only person making such a declaration.
Many people in our country are quietly deciding that they are "done
with church," and, when we try to figure out why, we realize they
have a variety of reasons for jumping ship.

## Done with Church

Let me mention several reasons I think people are abandoning the church.

*The church is too institutional.* Some people are tired of the church being more concerned with "institutional things" than "spiritual things."

If I'm honest, I have to admit that I spent a good part of my ministry in denial, trying to deny that the church was an institution. I knew in my heart of hearts that it was, but it hurt me to think of the church as not much different than Macy's or McDonald's—trying to draw a crowd, trying to appeal to young people, trying to increase profits, trying to build and maintain buildings, and trying to be bigger and more successful than the church down the street. It cheapened both the church and my calling as a pastor to think of the church as a religious corporation.

But the church *is* an institution, and, though it still pains me to admit it, the modern church seems to have more in common with big business than it does with its first-century prototype. Those early Christians, meeting in homes to eat, pray, sing, and celebrate, had little in common with we modern Christians building our multi-million-dollar buildings and hiring our mega-bucks pastors. We might look back at that simple, contagious church in Acts wistfully and even preach sermons extolling its virtues, but most churches have no intention of going back to that kind of faith community.

Some Christians are sensing, though, that the church is not supposed to be a religious version of Macy's or McDonald's and are turning their backs on it. They would like to find, or establish, a church that is less consumed with keeping itself alive, as all institutions must be, and more concerned with giving itself away. They find the Acts church more appealing than the McDonald's church.

*The church is too boring.* Others are "done with church" because the church has become boring to them. They have heard the same Sunday school lessons and sermons so long, sung the same hymns or praise choruses so often, and served on the same church committees for so many years that church has lost its intrigue. They've "been there and done that" and no longer find the church scene attractive.

Butler Bass writes,

> Many people are just bored. They are bored with church-as-usual, church-as-club, church-as-entertainment, or church-as-work. Many of my friends, faithful churchgoers for decades, are dropping out because religion is dull, the purview of folks who never want to change or always want to fight about somebody else's sex life; they see the traditional denominations as full of Mrs. Grundy priggishness. On Sundays, other things are more interesting—the *New York Times*, sports, shopping, Facebook, family time, working in the garden, biking, hiking, sipping lattes at the local coffee shop, meeting up at the dog park, getting the kids to the soccer game. Or just working. With tough economic times, lots of people work on Sunday mornings, the traditional time to attend to religious obligations.[2]

Suffice it to say that, in our kind of world, where people have so many choices, the church exists in a competitive market. If the church is boring and priggish, people will opt to do something more enjoyable and fulfilling. We traditionalists are not happy about that, but that's reality, and we might as well face it.

A boring church, playing "old tapes" from the past and pretending the world hasn't changed, will likely be an empty, dying church.

*The church is too scandalous.* The reputation of the church has taken a major "hit" in the last twenty years. One scandal after another has arisen to tarnish the image of the church, and many people have become disillusioned in the process.

Catholic priests have sexually abused children, and the Catholic church has been dealing with lawsuits and bad press for years. Well-known television evangelists have been guilty of everything from sexual trysts to embezzling money, and the media has made sure we all know about their indiscretions. The church's battles over abortion, homosexuality, the environment, the role of women, music, and politics in general have made it seem contentious—and perhaps it is.

The general public has definitely gotten the idea that the church is not as stable and trustworthy as it used to be.

These church-at-large issues have hurt the church's reputation, for sure, but probably haven't done as much damage as *local* church scandals. It's one thing to read about a scandal in the world at large; it's another thing altogether to go through a scandal in your own church.

But it happens all too often. The pastor runs off with the church secretary. The church splits over some controversial issue. The church treasurer absconds with the morning offering. The church decides to fire a staff member. And on and on it goes. With every local church skirmish, someone heads out the back door, never to return again.

This disillusionment with the scandalous church has translated into disillusionment with the clergy as well. In 2010, only 53 percent of Americans said that ministers had "high or very high" ethical standards—a percentage drop of some fourteen points from a survey ten years earlier. They trusted grade-school teachers, police officers, doctors, and military leaders more than ministers. Clergy ranked with bankers as the profession seeing the greatest decline in the decade.[3]

The recent past has been tough on the church's image, and some people have decided to drop out of this scandalous church and try to build a spiritual life without it.

*The church is too contentious.* For some people, it's not just scandal that has sabotaged their love for church; it's the contentious spirit they have experienced there.

They thought the church would be "one in the Spirit, one in the Lord," until they attended their first church business meeting and experienced church conflict up close and personal. Or until they went to their first personnel committee meeting and heard the committee castigating the church staff. Or until they went through the building campaign and got squarely in the middle of the fight over the pipe organ.

Some people have endured enough church conflict to last a lifetime and have the scars to prove it. So they have opted to drop out and let others fight those battles.

Two old quips come to my mind as I think about the church squabbles I myself have observed and survived. One is the old saw that Jesus came preaching the kingdom of God but what came forth was the church. It's true: the church is not always synonymous with the kingdom, and the next fight over the color of the carpet in the fellowship hall will prove it.

The other is the little poem that goes: "To live above with saints we love . . . O, that will be glory. To live below with saints we know . . . well, that's another story." To live with angry, contentious fellow believers *is* another story, and some have decided they just can't take it any longer.

*The church is too eccentric.* That last ditty leads to a final reason some have opted to leave the church: they have run into some truly strange and eccentric people at church, people who are hard to live with. It's not just that these people are contentious; it's that they're . . . well, weird.

When I look back on my many years as a pastor, I realize how many outcasts and misfits we had in the churches I pastored. People who could not make it in the real world, people who couldn't hold a job or live in a family, would be welcomed in our church. And that's the way it should have been. Church is a place of grace, and grace has wide arms that embrace people who get turned aside everywhere else in our society.

But this wonderful aspect of church life does create a problem. It lets into the church some people who are . . . well, outcasts and misfits. The church ends up with more than its share of people who have a hard time fitting in, people who just can't get along with others.

On one hand, the church's mandate to be full of grace attracts people who might be rejected and ridiculed elsewhere. On the other hand, that mandate allows the church to be populated with people who are difficult and demanding. It's a classic "Catch-22" situation: if the church is as open and accepting as it should be, it will attract people who are destined to make others in the church miserable.

"Whosoever will may come" is a fine motto for the church. It is also a motto that guarantees that church life will be anything but peaceful and harmonious. Butt heads with those difficult church people long enough, and you just might decide that life is too short to spend your life wrangling with outcasts and misfits. You might decide that church is not the place of peace and harmony you thought it would be and decide to spend next Sunday morning at the beach.

When I think about those five factors, I can understand why church attendance is plummeting. When people see the church as institutional, boring, scandalous, contentious, or eccentric, they're liable to sleep in on Sunday morning, take the kids to the park, or drift down to Starbucks for a latte.

Butler Bass says,

> In previous generations, scholars referred to eleven o'clock on Sunday morning as the most segregated hour in America, meaning that white people went to one church, black people to another. Now, the line of segregation is between those who go to church and those who do not. And, judging, by the number of cars parked in driveways on Sunday morning in most American cities and suburbs, it is not hard to figure out which group is growing.[4]

Little did I know that I would one day be in that growing group of non-churchgoers. Little did I know that I would one day find myself on the outside of the church looking in, seeing the church not through the eyes of a paid salesman but through the eyes of a wary customer.

## Tales of a Lifelong Churchman

Up until two years ago, I had been in church all my life. My parents attended a Baptist church and took me with them from the time I was born. I literally grew up in the church and was one of those people at church every time the doors were open.

We went to Sunday school, morning worship, Training Union, and evening worship on Sundays. Then on Wednesdays, I went to Royal Ambassadors and the midweek service. I also attended Vacation Bible School every summer, revivals twice a year, and Christian camps on a regular basis. Mention any activity or service in Baptist life, and I've attended it.

Then, when I graduated from high school, I went off to the world's largest Baptist university—Baylor—and joined a church near campus, until I was hired as a part-time music minister at the

Northcrest Baptist Church just north of Waco. Every Sunday, I taught a Sunday school class and then led the music at the morning and evening worship services. On Wednesday nights, I led our robust choir of eight in a rehearsal of the songs we would sing the next Sunday.

When I graduated from Baylor, I married Sherry, and, as newlyweds, we moved to Fort Worth so I could attend seminary. We joined a church there, until I became the pastor of a Baptist church in central Texas at the thriving metropolis of Andice, population 55. Every weekend, Sherry and I drove 170 miles to Andice, visited parishioners on Saturday, led the morning and evening services on Sunday, and returned to Fort Worth late Sunday night. For our efforts and our 340-mile round trip, we made a whopping $50 a week.

After seminary, we moved on to the Texas Baptist Children's Home in Round Rock for just over two years, where I served as chaplain and led the education program and worship services there. I was, in effect, the pastor of the children, cottage parents, and other workers at the children's home.

In 1977, we moved to the Houston area to begin a new church— the Heritage Park Baptist Church near NASA. We stayed there twenty years as the church grew from infancy to become a strong, flourishing congregation. I preached twice and sometimes three times every Sunday, led our midweek service, did funerals and weddings, and spent more time under the steeple than I care to remember.

I finished my pastoral career in San Antonio at the Woodland Baptist Church, where I served as pastor for thirteen years. Woodland was a suburban church filled with interesting, creative people. I performed all of my pastoral duties there—preaching, doing weddings and funerals, overseeing the staff, writing books and articles, and doing a lot of pastoral care to an aging congregation—with as much skill and enthusiasm as I could. At the end of 2010, I retired from Woodland, feeling good about my time there and my thirty-eight years as a pastor.

Looking back on it now, I realize that I was in church just about every Sunday for sixty-two years. And I was a "paid salesman" for the church for thirty-eight of those years. It was a good life, filled with joy and fine memories, and I am grateful for it. When I look back on all those years in the church, I do so with few regrets.

But when I retired at the tender age of sixty-two, for the first time in my life I didn't have to go to church on Sunday. It was a strange feeling, that first Sunday of retirement, to wake up and not have to go to church. I remember feeling relieved and guilty at the same time. Relieved because I didn't have to preach or bear the burden of leading a worship service. And guilty because I felt so free and happy not to have to go to church.

Since then, Sherry and I have attended a few Presbyterian churches, a Methodist church, an Episcopalian church, and a few Baptist churches. I have also preached on several occasions. We've also used our Sundays to hike, have breakfast out, travel, and take care of our grandsons.

We're not in "the church business" anymore and find ourselves more in the role of customers than salespeople. We have a different perspective on church now, and it has been a new and sometimes uncomfortable experience. But in this time of transition I've come to understand better why some people don't attend church. Viewing church from the perspective of a customer, I see things now that I never saw when I was a pastor.

Sherry and I used to see people out walking on Sunday morning, or riding their bikes, or working in their yard, and we would say, as we drove by them on our way to church, "These people aren't really happy. They might look happy. But they can't be happy without God and church in their lives."

We said it jokingly, of course, but deep down we wanted to believe it. We wanted to think that only those of us who would get up and go to church, those of us seriously cultivating our spiritual lives, were truly on the road to happiness.

I am here to report, now that I'm on this side of the fence, that those people probably *are* happy. They're happy pagans. Or happy lapsed church members. But they're quite content, thank you, without church.

And they see no compelling reason to give up their enjoyable Sunday routine to attend Sunday school or go to worship. Now that

I have walked a mile in their shoes, I *get* it. I've spent more than a few Sundays walking in their shoes, and I'm starting to understand unchurched people better than I ever have.

## Reaching the Introverts and Intellectuals

I think it is true that church attendance is unappealing to many people in our world, but I've come to see that attending church is especially unappealing for people who happen to be in one of two groups. If a person happens to be either introverted or intellectual, that person is destined to find church an especially inhospitable place.

As I mentioned back in chapter 1, introverts will feel out of place at church because church is structured for extroverts. When I try to appraise my reluctance to plug back into church, I know it has something to do with my introversion.

In her book *Leaving Church*, Barbara Brown Taylor writes about her own reluctance to return to the public eye after resigning as pastor of an Episcopal church in Georgia:

> I had thought I would be ready to get back to work by December, but I was wrong. I so loved the rhythm of waking with the sun, working at my own speed, and taking time to visit the chickens every day that the thought of keeping a schedule again filled me with dread. After so many weeks removed from public view, I also shrank from the prospect of being looked at again. Perhaps only deep introverts or people recovering from long illnesses can grasp such reticence, but it really does take a lot of energy to withstand human inspection.[5]

I'm sure that is part of my reluctance, too. I really don't want to be inspected again. I like being on this side of the periscope—looking at other people but not being looked at myself.

Extroverted pastors who have been on stage all their lives probably miss the limelight once they retire. Introverted pastors who have been on stage all their lives are thrilled not to be inspected anymore. And the thought of stepping back onto the stage—even in a bit part while sitting on a back pew—is not enticing.

But even people who are not pastors or church leaders have to be inspected when they come to church. They have to greet people during the passing of the peace, walk forward at the end of the service to join the church, stand up publicly to be baptized, or participate in a discussion in a Sunday school class. For extroverts, those are easy, even exciting, events. For introverts, they're the stuff of dread and dismay. And they just might be enough to keep them from going to church at all.

Intellects, too, suffer at church. By intellects, I'm referring to people who want to think "outside the box," ask serious and honest questions, and are capable of handling mystery and paradox. These cerebral types often find church too black-and-white and simplistic for their tastes.

Because churches are institutions, intent on growing larger, reaching the most people possible, and being institutionally successful, they have to pitch their message at a level that will appeal to the largest number of people in our society. If most people, let us say, are capable of a level two spirituality, a level two understanding of God, and a level two interpretation of Scripture, then the church will pitch its message at level two. If the church wants to grow and reach a large number of people, it will *have to* pitch its message at level two.

Those people who have advanced to level three or four spiritually will be consistently frustrated. They will find church to be dull, predictable, and less than stimulating. They might even say the church is dishonest or irrelevant. We can only hope they will find a church somewhere that will meet their intellectual needs and that they will continue to mature spiritually.

When I was a pastor, I used to ache for those introverts and intellects who would come to our church and never quite find a niche. Because our church, and every church, had to appeal to the masses to grow, those people not "in the masses" got left out.

Someday God might call me to begin the Introverts Baptist Church or maybe the Intellects Church of Honest Inquiry. We might not become a mega-church, but I'll bet we'll attract a loyal crowd.

As Sherry and I contemplate our future, we think that we will find our way back to church—probably sooner rather than later. We have been church people all our lives. We love the church. And we think church serves some important functions in our lives. We miss the corporate worship, the fellowship with Christian friends, and the tangible opportunities the church provides us to give and serve. Frankly, we don't miss being inspected, dealing with pettiness and conflict, and having to attend countless meetings.

But in the meantime, we will be careful observers, visit a variety of churches, try to discern on what "normal people" do and feel on a typical Sunday morning, and hope God can use all of that to teach and change us. And we wonder, as we talk about our future on our long walks on Sunday morning, how the church will have to change to appeal to wayward people like us.

## The Fourth Great Awakening?

All of this may sound negative and foreboding. Am I suggesting that the church is doomed to fail and that church people are riding an ecclesiastical *Titanic?* Is the church going under?

Though I have never claimed prophecy as one of my spiritual gifts, I will venture an educated guess: No, the church is not going under. However, I do think it is possible that the church *as we have always known it* is going under. I think it is possible, even probable, that the church model I grew up with and lived with all my life is being replaced by a new model. And that makes me both nervous and hopeful.

When I look around, I see changes that have happened in the world of commerce that I never would have imagined even a few years ago. "Big-box" department stores like Sears and J. C. Penney are suffering and shutting their doors. "Big-box" bookstores like Borders and Barnes & Noble are suffering, too, and giving way to Internet bookstores. Circuit City is gone, and Best Buy is downsizing its stores in response to online competition. The computer has changed everything in our society—for better or worse—and stores and businesses that were successful in the past are now fragile and failing.

The church I grew up with and pastored all of my life was a "big-box" model of church. It was patterned after some of the most successful businesses and corporations in America, and it worked for decades.

It featured big buildings, a staff of trained professionals, attractive programming, and such corporate staples as bylaws, budgets, marketing strategies, and advertising. It was a model that worked for a long time, and the big-business model for churches still reigns supreme in our country. Even churches in America that are small are not small on purpose, and they are trying desperately to grow and be a "big-box" success.

But the "big-box" model seems to be running out of steam. Just as J. C. Penney and Best Buy are finding the "big-box" model to be failing in the business world, so it seems that First Church is discovering that the "big-box" model is failing in the ecclesiastical world, too. Older members are becoming disillusioned with it, and young people are avoiding it like it is an irrelevant relic. First Church is being forced to take a long, hard look at how it does church in this new day.

So I don't think the church is going under; I just think that it is being forced to review its mission and revise its strategy. And I think the dissatisfaction with the church and anxiety about the church can and will lead the church to a new day, a day of fresh energy and focus. If the old model is dying, it may well be because a new church is waiting to be resurrected on the third day.

A writer named William McLoughlin wrote a small book years ago titled *Revivals, Awakenings, and Reform.* In that book, he suggests that North American Christianity entered a new period of awakening, a fourth Great Awakening in American history, around 1960. He said that this fourth Great Awakening continues to this day, and that we are living through one of the most eventful, though tumultuous, times in our country's religious history.[6]

Many writers today are trumpeting the advent of "the emerging church" or the "postmodern church," which is unlike the old "big-box" model and more open to questions, dialogue with other religions, and less structured worship and organization. Phyllis Tickle, former religion editor of *Publishers Weekly,* has said the church is in the midst of a major shift, the kind of shift that happens only once every five hundred years or so.

However it is described, anyone close to the church today senses that major changes are taking place. The tremors are already shaking the foundations, and we're not exactly sure what is going to happen next. We only know that the tremors are both terrifying and exciting.

With all of the faith I have, I trust that a good, gracious God is sovereign over this transformation. This shaking of the foundations *is* frightening, and we grieve over the empty pews in our churches and the number of young adults who are staying away in droves. That feels like failure to us, and we American Christians certainly don't like to fail.

But in our death there will be resurrection. God will do a new thing. A new version of the church will rise from the ashes of our "big-box" buildings. And our children and grandchildren will meet God in church—perhaps a newer, more vibrant version of church than we have today.

## For Reflection or Discussion

1. When you hear the word "church," do you have positive or negative feelings? Why?

2. Do you think the church is losing its influence in our society? Why or why not?

3. Do you know people who are "done with church"? What brought them to that decision?

4. What can the church do to reclaim its deserters? What can it do to reach new people with the gospel?

5. Does your church have its share of eccentric people, people who are hard to get along with? How does it handle these people?

6. Have you ever wandered away from church? What brought you back?

7. Are you thinking of wandering away from church right now? What has brought on your disillusionment?

8. How can the church reach introverts and intellectuals? Or should it aim its message and ministries at the broadest segment of the population?

9. Is our country in the midst of a Great Awakening? Or is it drifting further and further away from God?

## NOTES

1. Diana Butler Bass, *Christianity After Religion: The End of Church and the Birth of a New Spiritual Awakening*, digital version (New York: HarperOne, 2012) location 232.

2. Ibid., location 260.

3. Gallup, "Honesty/Ethics in Professions," 19–21 November 2010, www.gallup.com.

4. Butler Bass, *Christianity After Religion*, location 267.

5. Barbara Brown Taylor, *Leaving Church* (San Francisco: HarperSanFrancisco, 2006) 196.

6. William McLoughlin, *Revivals, Awakenings, and Reform: An Essay on Religion and Social Change in America, 1607–1977* (Chicago: University of Chicago Press, 1978).

# CHAPTER 6

# Gambling on God
## (Why Do I Have So Many Doubts?)

In his book *Wishful Thinking*, Frederick Buechner writes, "Whether your faith is that there is a God or that there is not a God, if you don't have any doubts you are either kidding yourself or asleep. Doubts are the ants in the pants of faith. They keep it awake and moving."[1]

As a person who has had, and still has, more than his share of doubts, I find that comforting. I would like to think that my doubts are a sign of honesty and that they do indeed keep me awake and moving. I would like to wear my doubts as a badge of integrity.

But if doubts are the ants in the pants of faith, we should at least admit that ants are a painful nuisance. Ants can make your life miserable. They can ruin your picnic. They can bring your children to tears. They can—and this has happened to me on more than one occasion—short out your air-conditioning system. The truth is, few of us have a favorable impression of ants. They are never mentioned on anyone's list of favorite creatures.

So let's admit that doubts, too, are a painful nuisance. They destroy our confidence. They creep into our minds and make us miserable. They cause us to remain silent in our Sunday school class or Bible study group. Even if we try to put a positive spin on the existence of our doubts, we would just as soon not have them, and we find ourselves envious of our Christian friends who are brimming with certainty. Doubts, like ants, are a pain.

But some of us are afflicted with doubts and can't seem to avoid them. For that reason, my favorite disciple has long been Thomas, who refused to believe in the risen Jesus until he had tangible proof: "Unless I see the mark of the nails in his hands, and put my finger in the mark of the nails and my hand in his side, I will not believe" (John 20:25).

Thomas didn't want to believe on the basis of hearsay. He didn't want to get caught up in mass delusion. He didn't want to commit his life to something or someone unless he had solid evidence. I'm the same way, so I've admired Thomas's kind of faith for a long time.

I don't want to believe in God because others do; I want to believe in God because it makes sense to do so and because the existence of God is more likely than the absence of God.

I don't want to believe in the Bible just because others do; I want to believe in the Bible because I've read it myself, tested its truths, and found them credible.

I don't want to go to church because others do; I want to go to church because church is an honest, loving community that makes an eternal difference in the world.

I don't want to bear witness for Christ because I've been told I should; I want to bear witness for Christ because he really is the way, the truth, and the life and because following him will lead my family and friends to abundant living.

In short, I don't want to be a Christian because it's the way I was raised, because everyone around me claims to be a Christian, or because people are willing to pay me to preach or write books about Christianity. I want to be a Christian because the Christian Way is true and because it leads me to the God of the universe.

What that has meant for me is a life full of questioning and probing—and yes, doubting. I have always had more than my share of spiritual ants, so I feel eminently qualified to write about doubt.

Let me mention several truths I have learned as I have grappled with doubt in my own life.

## A Normal Component of Faith

The first thing I would mention is that *doubt is a normal component of faith*. Perhaps it would be more accurate to say that doubt is a normal component of *my* faith or *some people's* faith. I have known many Christians for whom doubt is not an issue at all. They believe the

Bible, trust in God, serve faithfully in the church, and never once have a doubt about anything. They would read this chapter and wonder why in the world I don't just quit questioning things and live with faith. They're quite content to say, "God said it; I believe it; that settles it."

But for some of us poor, skeptical types, that approach to the Christian life just won't work. We're envious of (and sometimes perturbed at) those who can have such a simple, trusting faith, but we can't in good conscience work up that kind of faith ourselves. We question and doubt, and, if we have faith at all, it often seems even smaller than the proverbial mustard seed Jesus requires.

We silently wonder about certain parts of Scripture, though we can't afford to voice our concerns to any of the Christians we know.

We look at the people around us and notice that non-Christians seem to be as kind, loving, and godly as people in the church.

We read of natural disasters and unthinkable atrocities and wonder how a loving God could allow such things to happen.

We cringe when we watch the silly antics of "true believers" and want to shout to the world, "But I'm not like them!"

We fidget through church on Sunday morning, put off by the trumped-up emotionalism in the worship service and the trite, formulaic sermon the pastor delivers.

In these and many other ways, we are out of step with our Christian brothers and sisters. We're skeptics and cynics and can't seem to help it.

What's wrong with us, anyway? Why can't we just have faith? Why can't we just believe?

I would like to think that there's nothing wrong with us. We simply want to have an honest faith. We're the descendants of Thomas who refuse to believe without proof. We're the people who would rather have no faith at all than a faith we believe is a lie.

It seems to me that doubt is a natural component of faith. We do not walk by sight, though we would love to. We would love to see signs, wonders, and miracles. We would love to hear the audible voice of God (more about this shortly).

But we don't walk by sight; we walk by faith. That means that we don't have all the answers we want, that we walk in semi-darkness most of the time, and that we question and probe. And that questioning and probing doesn't feel like sin to us; it feels like trying to be honest to and with God.

## A Result of Passion

This I believe, too: *doubt is a result of passion.* By that, I mean we doubt because we care so much about God, because we refuse to be casual about spiritual matters.

My children were athletes when they were in high school. My daughter, Stacy, played volleyball and basketball and ran track. My son, Randel, was a wide receiver on the football team. When they were playing sports in high school, Sherry and I were consumed with their athletic events.

We went to all of their games and meets. We served in the booster club. I subscribed to both Houston newspapers and checked them daily, hoping to see Stacy's or Randel's name in the sports page. When our kids were in high school, we lived and breathed sports.

But, to my embarrassment, I also suffered more than I should have during those days. If Stacy wasn't hitting her three-point shots or Randel dropped a pass or two, I tossed and turned at night, unable to sleep.

Often, I silently berated their coaches. Why couldn't the basketball coach see that she needed to build her team around Stacy? And why couldn't the football coach see that Randel needed to have more passes thrown his way? If the team did well and my kids were the stars, I was a happy man. But if the team was slumping and my kids were not playing well, I was not fun to be around.

Looking back on those days now, I realize how silly and foolish it was to invest so much of my emotional energy on high schoolers playing games. But if I have an excuse, here it is: I worried, lost sleep, and played the fool because I was so passionate about sports and, more important, about my children. My silly, irrational actions were connected to my irrational love for Stacy and Randel and my desire that they succeed in their athletic endeavors.

I have come to see my doubts the same way. My doubts and questions about God, the Bible, the church, and spirituality stem from my passion. I am not casual about God. I cannot act like these things don't matter. I must know the truth, even if that means tossing and turning at night, wrestling with unseen angels (or demons!).

John Suk is the pastor of a Christian Reformed Church in Canada and the author of a book titled *Not Sure (A Pastor's Journey from Faith to Doubt)*. The book is a chronicle of his struggle to believe, to be orthodox, and to be honest. At one point in the book, he writes,

> I suppose it must seem odd to most people that faith—or lack of it—can rile me up so much. Why not get exercised, instead, over how the Blue Jays or my mutual funds are doing? I don't know. Sometimes I wish baseball were my passion. In my religious life, I wish I could get up on Sunday mornings, pull the tie tight around my neck, march off to church, and sing at the top of my lungs while never giving anything but God's grace a second thought. But I can't. And sometimes, given the culture I grew up in and the certainty of so many professional religious people around me, I have even wondered whether my doubt disqualifies my faith and brings my leadership roles in my Christian community into doubt. Sometimes I wonder whether or not I'm a hypocrite.[2]

I'm sure there are Christians who would declare him a hypocrite and consider him unfit to be a pastor. They would say his doubt disqualifies him from preaching. How can a "doubting Thomas" ever hope to speak a confident word of challenge or comfort to anyone?

But, as for me, I would rather have a pastor like Suk than one who sees the world, God, and life only in black and white. I do not want a pastor unacquainted with life's ambiguities and unable to recognize gray. I would rather have an honest pastor with doubts than a dishonest pastor with certainty.

Doubt, I think, is always connected to passion. We doubt because we care. We care too much about God to describe him in three points that all begin with the same letter. We care too much about the Bible to try to tame its wild wisdom and turn it into a self-help manual. We care too much about prayer to reduce it to a spiritual slot machine.

And we care too much about the people around us to condemn them to hell just because they don't believe exactly like we do.

In short, we care too much *not* to doubt. And while we might envy our brothers and sisters shouting, "God said it; I believe it; that settles it," in truth, we would not swap places with them.

At least we have "the ants in the pants of faith" that keep us asking, seeking, and knocking. At least we care enough to doubt.

## The Silence of God

Let's acknowledge, too, that *doubt is connected to the silence of God.* Don't you wish God would just come out and say something? Don't you wish God would give you just one Damascus Road experience? Don't you long for a time when God knocks you down, speaks audibly to you, and once and for all removes all doubt from your mind?

If we could only have a moment like that, we would astound the world with our faith. Peter and Paul would seem like spiritual midgets compared to us. Nothing could stop us, and no one could quell our passion. After we were long dead and gone, people would write books about our amazing lives, lived to the glory of God.

But most of us never get that kind of experience. We live on hints and hunches. We trust the wisdom of our parents and teachers. We listen to preachers and professors and hope they are telling us the truth. But we never get a Damascus Road experience, and, because we never get the direct, dramatic revelation we crave, we sometimes find ourselves doubting it all.

What if our hints and hunches are wrong? What if our parents and teachers, for all of their good intentions, are just parroting what their parents and teachers told them? What if our preachers and professors are giving us the denominational "party line," a line they have blindly believed all their lives? What if, in other words, our faith is "small town" in a "large city" world?

That is the risk we all run. And that is why we would love for God to say something for a change. Say something, God, so we can know the truth. Say something, God, and deliver us from our deceptions. Say something, God, and remove the gray from our experience.

We are certainly not the first believers to voice those requests. David in the psalms often complained about the mystifying silence of God, a silence that battered him into both anger and submission.

Anselm, an eleventh-century theologian, once wrote, "I have never seen thee, O Lord my God; I do not know thy form. . . . What shall thy servant do, anxious in his love of thee, and cast out afar from thy face? He pants to see thee, and thy face is too far from him. He longs to come to thee, and thy dwelling place is inaccessible. . . . Heavy loss, heavy grief, heavy all our fate!"[3]

Of course, one dishonest thing we can do in light of our "heavy loss, heavy grief, and heavy fate" is fake it. We can act as if God *has* spoken to us and pretend that we *have* heard a voice on the road to Damascus.

Suk writes about this almost universal desire we have to hear and experience God:

> You can't argue with people who say they've experienced a spirit guide from a past life, or who say they had a near-death experience of an angel leading them up, up, and away. You can't argue with people who go to an evangelical church and say that Jesus revealed to them that they should take a new job or pray for a friend. Religious people, regardless of their specific faith, always claim such things. And that's how it is in postmodern North America. Whatever our institutional religion, and whatever creeds and confessions we nominally hold to, what most of us want is an excellent spiritual experience.[4]

If we can just have an excellent spiritual experience, we won't have to doubt anymore. We will have heard and seen God and be able to walk through life with serene confidence.

But if God is silent, mysterious, and hard to know, then doubt is normal and not surprising. We're trying to relate to Someone we can't see, hear, or even fathom, and that makes doubt our constant companion.

# Not a Choice

Those of us afflicted with these irritating theological ants have to say, too, that *doubt is not a choice*. To people who wonder why we doubters don't just quit doubting and start showing some faith for a change, my answer is that I don't choose to doubt. I have never once said, "I think I'll start doubting God. I think I'll spite my family, my theology professors, and my heritage and become a skeptic." Doubt showed up in my life uninvited, and I have had to learn to deal with it.

Suk writes,

> Doubt is not a choice. I have not chosen doubt as a way to strike back at former colleagues or verities or at institutions where I have worked. No, doubt is a virus: you catch it without knowing where you caught it. There are very few, if any, effective treatments, and it can be painful and debilitating. Doubt may go into remission, but it is chronic and may flare up anytime. As Voltaire famously put it, "Doubt is not a pleasant condition, but certainty is absurd."[5]

Those afflicted with the doubt virus are not typically popular in evangelical circles. Let's face it: people don't want to be around someone with a virus. Doubters have a way of raining on the parade of others and can ruin a perfectly good prayer group or Bible study class.

So those of us afflicted with the doubt virus tend to stay quiet in such settings. We really don't want to rain on anyone's parade, and we really don't want to give our doubt to anyone else. Better, then, to keep our doubts to ourselves.

If you are afflicted with the doubt virus, my condolences go out to you. Your disease can be painful and debilitating. But my congratulations go out to you, too, for you will keep asking, seeking, and knocking, and you will learn new and important truths in your searching.

The ants will make you miserable, but they will also keep your faith awake and moving.

# An Attempt to Understand

It might be obvious, but it is also worth mentioning that *doubt is an honest attempt to understand.* We doubt because "now we see though a mirror dimly" (1 Cor 13:12), and we would like to get a better view of God, ourselves, and the world.

When we doubt, we acknowledge our fallibility and humanity. We're admitting we don't have all the answers (and that some of the answers we thought we had have turned out to be wrong), but we want to keep discovering. We want to grow "in grace and knowledge" (2 Pet 3:18).

Doubters at least have a chance of moving beyond superficial spirituality. If we don't ask, seek, and knock, we can end up with a faith that is about as deep as a roadside puddle. If we decide to cast our lot with popular religion, with its bumper-sticker theology and emotional hysteria, we will be on a broad road traveled by many people.

But popular religion produces shallow people. Several years ago, Bill McKibben wrote an article in *Harper's* magazine that described the current condition of American Christianity:

> Only 40 percent of Americans can name more than four of the Ten Commandments, and a scant half can cite any of the four authors of the Gospels. Twelve percent believe Joan of Arc was Noah's wife. This failure to recall the specifics of our Christian heritage may be further evidence of our nation's educational decline, but it probably doesn't matter all that much in spiritual or political terms. Here is a statistic that does matter: Three quarters of Americans believe the Bible teaches that, "God helps those who help themselves." That is, three out of four Americans believe that this uber-American idea, a notion at the core of our current individualist politics and culture, which was in fact uttered by Ben Franklin, actually appears in Holy Scripture. The thing is, not only is Franklin's wisdom not biblical; it's counterbiblical. Few ideas could be further from the gospel message, with its radical summons to love of neighbor. On this essential matter, most Americans—most American Christians—are simply wrong, as if 75 percent of American scientists believed that Newton proved gravity causes apples to fly up.[6]

In that kind of ignorant culture, don't you think some people should be doubting? Doesn't it make sense that a few people should question the status quo? McKibben's article was titled "The Christian Paradox: How a Faithful Nation Gets Jesus Wrong." If our faithful nation gets Jesus wrong on this one point, how many other points is it getting wrong? And shouldn't a few skeptics arise to get us back on track?

So let us doubt. Let us not blindly accept the Christian status quo. Let us keep doubting and questioning until we get it right. And, even if we never get it exactly right, maybe we'll at least learn the difference between Jesus and Ben Franklin.

## A Happy Ending

Finally, I want to affirm that *doubts can have a happy ending.* We fear those nasty ants in the pants of faith because their bite just might be fatal. That has likely happened to some believers. They once believed in God, but then doubt did its dastardly work, and they became unbelievers. Their faith was eaten up by ants.

But my guess is that those people are few and far between. They are the exception to the rule. What happens more often is that doubters wake up and start to move. Their doubts keep them searching, and they end up with a more mature, fulfilling faith than they would have had without their doubts.

In other words, their doubts take them not to defection but to maturity. They go from a level one or two on the spirituality scale to a level of three or four. Their doubts season their lives and enhance their wisdom.

I would like to think something like that has happened to me. I know my doubts have changed me; I can only hope and pray that the changes are for the better.

I once had a God who was stern and strict . . . until I started to doubt that concept of God. Now my God is full of love and grace, and my dread is gone.

I once had a Bible that was a rulebook of moral truth . . . until I started to doubt that concept of the Bible. Now my Bible is a treasure chest of wisdom from a variety of God-seekers who were seeking God in their own time and place.

I once viewed prayer as a way to ask God for favors . . . until I started to doubt that concept of prayer. Now prayer is a way of staying in touch with God so I can change and grow.

I once had a church that could be measured in buildings, budgets, and baptisms . . . until I started to doubt that concept of church. Now my church is measured in friendships, truth, and acts of love.

I once saw the Christian life as bad news, as checking boxes on an offering envelope to prove my devotion to God . . . until I started to doubt that concept of the Christian life. Now the Christian life is good news, and I am filled with gratitude for what God has done for me in Christ.

When I look back at my own spiritual journey, I think I see the value of doubt. Because the virus struck me at a fairly early age, I started questioning God, the Bible, prayer, the church, and the Christian life, and "all things became new." I'm a very different kind of Christian now than I was before I had my doubts, and, though many of my more fundamentalist friends might not agree, I think I am a *better* kind of Christian.

On those days when doubt threatens to overwhelm me, when God seems distant, the Bible a barbaric book from the hands of ancient people, and prayer a futile exercise in wishful thinking, I think about a passage in John's Gospel. In John 6, Jesus has been talking about his coming death, and many people are defecting as a result of his teachings. Jesus turns to his disciples and asks them if they wish to leave, too.

Simon Peter answers and says, "Lord, to whom can we go? You have the words of eternal life. We have come to believe and know that you are the Holy One of God" (John 6:68-69).

In essence, Peter was saying, "Jesus, we don't understand all that you are saying and all that is happening to us. But where else can we turn? Who has a better plan for us? We've been around you enough to know that you are for real and that you are from God. I, for one, am staying because I can't think of a better person to trust."

That passage reminds me of something Lewis Smedes wrote in his book *My God and I: A Spiritual Memoir:* "Without Jesus we are stuck with utopian illusion or deadly despair. I scorn illusion. I dread despair. So I put my money on Jesus."[7]

On those days when doubt is especially oppressive, I find myself saying the same thing. I might be beset with doubt, I certainly don't have all the answers, and God often seems far, far away. But so far, I'm with Peter and Lewis Smedes.

In the face of doubt, I put my money on Jesus.

## Examining the Tool Kit

When we were born, each of us was handed a spiritual tool kit. We have used that tool kit all of our lives to fashion an understanding of and relationship to God. Tool kits vary from person to person, depending on things like where you were born and who your parents happened to be.

When I think about my personal tool kit, I see it had the following characteristics: it was *American*; it was American *Christian*; it was American *evangelical* Christian; it was American *Baptist* evangelical Christian; it was American *fundamentalist* Baptist evangelical Christian.

Because I was handed an American fundamentalist Baptist evangelical Christian tool kit, it was filled with an assortment of tools: Sunday school, Vacation Bible School, revivals, Training Union, Lay Renewal weekends, summer camps, Royal Ambassadors, Wednesday night suppers, prayer meetings, emotional preaching, and probably a hundred other activities and events. The purpose of every tool in my kit was the same: to introduce me to God and help me love and serve him.

Had I been born a Hindu in India, a Buddhist in Japan, or even a Catholic in New York, I would have been given a very different tool kit. I am who I am today, and I believe what I believe today, because of the tool kit my family handed me when I was born.

Though I am certainly not an objective evaluator, I think it was a wonderful tool kit. I have always been proud of my spiritual heritage and grateful for those who taught and trained me in the Southern Baptist way of thinking and living.

But I also know that my tool kit is not perfect. As I have gotten older, I've been able to look at some of the things I was taught and some of the activities I participated in and realize that my tool kit is not inerrant. Along with love and grace, my tool kit also had its fair share of guilt, manipulation, pressure, emotionalism, and spiritual haughtiness. I've been forced to look at some of the things in my tool kit and toss them away.

And make no mistake: Tossing things out of your spiritual tool kit is painful. It feels like turning your back on your past and on the people who nurtured you. It feels like a loss of faith, when, in reality, it is a step toward more mature faith. But when you're tossing tools out of your kit, it feels like you're rejecting your past—which, I suppose, you are.

But tossing tools out of our spiritual tool kits and replacing them with better, more useful tools is the essence of spiritual growth. And doubt is the ingredient that enables us to get on with this valuable work. When we doubt, we're looking long and hard at our tools and trying to decide which ones work and which ones don't.

In his book *The Truing of Christianity*, John C. Meagher writes,

> Over the years, I have thought, and then dropped, approximately thirty-seven editions of God. I have cringed before some of them, manipulated others, defied a few, ignored some, and in a few cases tried to think about it as little as possible, for fear that God would disappear. I don't miss them. I now feel persuaded that God will not disappear, whatever may happen to my current and future editions, and I want to think about God in a way that will take that into account: what would it be like to think about God in a way that will not collapse under inspection, that can face up to everything and stand in all weather?[8]

Isn't that what we all want? Don't we want a concept of God that will not collapse under inspection? And doesn't that mean changing our current understanding of God to embrace an even better understanding of God?

I think it does. But I think we'll never get there unless we doubt. I think we'll never move and change until the ants start to bite.

## For Reflection or Discussion

1. Are doubts "the ants in the pants of faith" that enable us to grow? Or are they evil thoughts that ruin our faith?

2. Have you ever had doubts about God, the Bible, your salvation, or the church? What did you do with those doubts?

3. What can the church do to face and address the doubts people have? Is your church a safe place for doubters or a condemning place?

4. Is doubt a result of spiritual passion or a sign of spiritual stagnation? Has doubt helped or hurt your own spiritual development?

5. Has the silence of God ever bothered you? Have you longed for clearer, more direct revelation from God?

6. If you are assailed by doubts, what basic truths or experiences keep you tethered to God?

### NOTES

1. Frederick Buechner, *Wishful Thinking* (New York: Harper & Row, 1973) 20.

2. John Suk, *Not Sure* (Grand Rapids: Eerdmans, 2011) 120.

3. Quoted in Suk, *Not Sure*, 143.

4. Ibid., 106.

5. Ibid., 6.

6. Bill McKibben, "The Christian Paradox: How a Faithful Nation Gets Jesus Wrong," *Harper's*, August 2005, www.harpers.org/archive/2005/0080695.

7. Lewis Smedes, *My God and I: A Spiritual Memoir* (Grand Rapids: Eerdmans, 2003), 177.

8. John Meagher, *The Truing of Christianity* (New York: Doubleday, 1990) 7–8.

# CHAPTER 7

# Of Airplanes and Sailboats

## *(How Can I Make Sense of Scripture?)*

Once upon a time, a young boy was given a model airplane kit for his birthday. He loved assembling model planes, and his room was filled with the planes he had built. But this particular airplane kit caused him a lot of problems.

For one thing, it didn't contain any instructions, so he knew that he would have to try to assemble the plane simply by looking at the picture on the box. For another thing, the pieces in the box were not like any pieces he had ever seen before. For the life of him, he couldn't find any wings or a fuselage or a cockpit. Obviously, this kit was going to present him with quite a challenge.

So he took all the pieces out of the box, laid them out on the floor, and pondered them. He noticed that one slender piece looked like a mast for a sail. Another piece looked like the hull of a boat. And still another colorful piece looked remarkably like a sail. Is it possible, he wondered, that what I have here is not an airplane but a sailboat? Could it be that the picture on the box is not an accurate representation of the pieces the box actually contains?

Once he realized he might be dealing with a sailboat instead of an airplane, he had no trouble building the boat. Even without instructions, he was astute enough to piece together the sailboat. And when he had finished it, he was even prouder of his new boat than he was of all the airplanes in his room.

I tell you that young boy's story because I think something like that has happened to most of us when it comes to understanding the

Bible. We've been told some specific things about the Bible, and we've spent a good portion of our lives trying to piece together a life built on biblical principles. But, try as we might, the Bible doesn't speak to us the way we want it to. We know it's supposed to be our handbook for living. We know other people testify to its wisdom and power. And we know it's supposed to be the very word of God to us. But, though we hate to admit it, the Bible often seems boring, dated, and difficult.

I want to suggest to you in this chapter that we've spent most of our lives trying to put together an airplane when, in reality, we're dealing with a sailboat. I think most of us have a picture of the Bible in our minds that is not accurate. We think we know what the Bible is and what it is supposed to do, but, in truth, the pieces in the box don't match our expectations.

When it comes to the Bible, we live in constant disappointment and disillusionment because we think it's an airplane when it's actually a sailboat. And if we would just realize that, then we could start making sense of Scripture and find it to be something far different and far better than we ever imagined.

## Understanding *Biblicism*

In his book *The Bible Made Impossible (Why Biblicism Is Not a Truly Evangelical Reading of Scripture)*, Christian Smith describes an approach to Scripture that he calls *biblicism*. His description of *biblicism* describes the way I was taught to believe about the Bible and, I'm guessing, the way nearly all evangelical Christians were taught to believe.

Smith says that *biblicism* is represented by ten assumptions or beliefs:

1. Divine Writing. The Bible is God's word, written inerrantly in human language.
2. Total Representation. The Bible is the totality of God's communication to humanity and contains all that God has to say to people.

3. Complete Coverage. The divine will about all of the issues relevant to Christian belief and life is contained in the Bible.

4. Democratic Perspicuity. Any reasonably intelligent person can
read the Bible in his or her own language and understand the plain
meaning of the text.

5. Commonsense Hermeneutics. The best way to understand biblical texts is by reading them in their explicit, plain, literal sense,
which may or may not involve taking into account literary, cultural,
and historical contexts.

6. *Solo Scriptura*. The significance of any biblical text can be
understood without reliance on any other source such as creeds,
confessions, or historical church traditions.

7. Internal Harmony. All related passages of the Bible on any given
subject fit together like puzzle pieces into a single, unified, consistent whole. Scripture never contradicts itself.

8. Universal Applicability. What the biblical writers taught at
any point in history remains universally valid for all Christians at
every other time, unless explicitly revoked by subsequent scriptural
teaching.

9. Inductive Method. All matters of Christian belief and practice
can be learned by sitting down with the Bible and piecing together
through careful study the truths that it teaches.

10. Handbook Model. The Bible teaches morals and doctrines with
every affirmation it makes, so that together these affirmations are a
handbook or textbook for Christian belief and living. The Bible is
a compendium of divine, infallible teachings about everything from
science and politics to romance and personal finance.[1]

Those ten assumptions or beliefs were never specifically articulated to
me, but they aptly capture the approach to the Bible I learned growing
up in the Baptist church. I grew up believing that all ten of those
things were true, and, in fact, that if anyone did not affirm any of
those things, then he or she had a faith that was suspect. I grew up
singing, "The B-I-B-L-E, that's the book for me. I stand alone on the
word of God. The B-I-B-L-E." That, I suppose, is *biblicism's* theme
song.

But, as I have studied the Bible through the years, I have come to
question some of *biblicism's* assertions. It's not that I doubt the Bible;

it's that I doubt the way I was taught to view the Bible. I have started to think that I was told I was working with an airplane when, in truth, I've always been building a sailboat.

Let's probe, then, some ways we might have approached Scripture with wrong expectations—what the Bible *is not*, and then turn our attention to perhaps a more accurate, honest way of approaching the Bible—what the Bible *is*.

## What the Bible Is Not

First, *the Bible is not a handbook for successful living.* Recently, I had a taillight bulb burn out in my car and needed to replace it. It seemed like a simple task, one that even a mechanically challenged person like me could handle. So I did what any person would do in that situation—I got out the car manual in the glove compartment, looked up "taillight bulb," and managed to do the job myself. Any time I need to do a minor repair job on the car, that manual is indispensable.

I grew up thinking the Bible was my handbook for living. If I needed to know anything about life—dating, money, contentment, relationships, or the end times—the Bible was the manual I was to use to "look up the answer" to my question. I saw the Bible as a kind of spiritual encyclopedia, chock full of answers if only I knew how and where to look.

When I look around me, I see that this is still the most common way people use the Bible. I see T-shirts and bumper stickers that say,

*God said it, I believe it, That settles it!*

*BIBLE—Basic Instruction Before Leaving Earth*

*Confused? Read the Directions* (picture of the Bible)

*Have Truth Decay? Brush Up on Your Bible*

I also see dozens of books that declare that the Bible is our handbook for living:

*Bible Answers for Almost All Your Questions*

*100 Biblical Tips to Help You Live a More Peaceful and Prosperous Life*

*Cooking with the Bible: Recipes for Biblical Meals*

*Bible Prophecy 101: A Guide to End Times in Plain Language*

*Handbook for Christian Living: Biblical Answers to Life's Tough Questions*

*Bible Solutions to Problems of Daily Living*

*God's Blueprint for Building Marital Intimacy*

*What the Bible Says about Parenting: Biblical Principles for Raising Godly Children*

*Getting the Skinny on Prosperity: Biblical Principles That Work for Everyone*

*Body by God: The Owner's Manual for Maximized Living*

That list could go on and on, and Christian Smith has a much longer list of such titles in his book. Suffice it to say that this "handbook, textbook, manual-for-living" approach to the Bible is the dominant one in our culture.

I have this picture in my mind, though, of some well-meaning, earnest seeker who wants advice on dealing with his rebellious teenage son. He has heard that the Bible has the answers to life's problems, so he buys a Bible and starts to read it for the first time in his life. He's ready to soak up the wisdom the Bible will impart to him as he tries to relate to his son.

But he's surprised at what he finds. He starts reading about Adam and Eve in the garden, moves on to Cain murdering Abel, and then sails into the story of Noah and the ark. He reads about the tower of Babel, the calling of Abram, and the sacrificing of Isaac at the altar.

He keeps plowing through Genesis, waiting to get to the advice for parents who are dealing with rebellious children, but all he gets is this strange story about people who lived in another time and place, a story that seems out of touch with his own life.

If he doesn't despair, that father will keep reading into Exodus and learn about Moses and the exploits of the Israelites as they journey to the promised land. Then he will get to Leviticus and start reading the strange laws and regulations God gave the people of Israel.

If he is unusually persistent, he will move on to Deuteronomy, where he will eventually get to a passage that says,

> If someone has a stubborn and rebellious son who will not obey his father and mother, who does not heed them when they discipline him, then his father and his mother shall take hold of him and bring him out to the elders of his town at the gate of that place. They shall say to elders of his town, "This son of ours is stubborn and rebellious. He will not obey us. He is a glutton and a drunkard." Then all of the men of the town shall stone him to death. So you shall purge the evil from your midst; and all Israel shall hear, and be afraid. (Lev 21:18-21)

He will read that passage again, not believing what he has just read. This is what the Bible teaches about dealing with your rebellious children? He's supposed to take his son to the city's elders and have him stoned to death? Though he has often been frustrated beyond belief at his son, he has never once considered stoning him. And now the Bible is advocating that as the solution to his parenting dilemma?

At that point, that father puts the Bible down and assumes one of two things. Either he has not understood the Bible at all, or the Bible is not the handbook of successful living people have told him it is. Something is seriously askew here. But this father puts his Bible aside and might, in fact, never refer to it again. It wasn't as helpful as advertised.

What has happened to that father, I think, is that he was looking for an airplane when he was actually dealing with a sailboat. Contrary to what our culture tells us, the Bible is not a manual for living. We don't go to it like I went to the car manual to fix my taillights or like we used to go to the encyclopedia to do our research papers in high school. That father's heart was definitely in the right place, but someone needed to tell him about the sailboat.

Someone needed to sit him down and tell him something like this: "The Bible is not a book of tips on successful living. It is a complicated story that is designed to show us our sin and God's solution to our sin, which is Jesus Christ. We don't go to the Bible to get inerrant answers to all of our questions. We go to the Bible to see how people through the ages have related to God and what God finally did to put us right with him. So keep reading past all of that strange stuff in Leviticus and Deuteronomy. Keep going until you get to 'in Christ God was reconciling the world to himself' (2 Cor 5:19). Then, soak yourself in the teachings of Jesus, and you will start to see some implications for the way you can relate to your son."

In *The Bible Made Impossible,* Christian Smith writes,

> The Bible is not about offering tips for living a good life. It is about Jesus Christ who is our only good and our only life. By ceasing to look to the Bible to answer inerrantly all of life's questions, we thus remove from the table the temptation to take definitive moral and theological stands on a number of issues that the Bible does not address. Such a view forces us to back up and approach some of those questions with a very different framework of inquiry—a gospel-centered, not a *biblicist,* framework.[2]

I have no doubt that the *biblicist* framework will continue to be the one most people in our culture will use when contemplating the Bible. But I also have no doubt that trying to make the Bible into a handbook for successful living is destined to frustrate people like that father in my illustration. Try as we might to make it into an airplane, the Bible is a sailboat. And we'll never fully understand or appreciate it until we let it be what it truly is.

Second, *the Bible is not the final word on all subjects.* To those of us schooled in *biblicism,* that might sound like heresy, but an honest look at the Bible will reveal it to be the case. The Bible simply refuses to answer all of our questions on all topics. Smith writes,

> It may be not only that God, in giving us the Bible, does not intend through it to inform us about topics like biblical cooking and stress management. It also may be that God does not even intend the

Bible to provide us with direct, specific, nonnegotiable instructions about things like church polity and government, the "end times," the ethics of war, divine foreknowledge, the "scientific" aspects of the Genesis creation, the correct modes of baptism, proper elements of correct Christian worship, the exact nature of sanctification, or the destiny of the unevangelized.[3]

Think, for a moment, how liberating it would be to let the Bible be what it is—a book written over a span of some two thousand years by over forty different men that reflects their understanding and experience of God, a book that also reflects their own time and place, a book never intended to be the final word on every topic of interest to people in the twenty-first century.

For me, that thought doesn't destroy biblical authority; it enhances it. It lets the Bible be what it really is—not a handbook or encyclopedia but a story of redemption and good news, a story primarily about Jesus Christ and what he came to be and do.

Consider, as you ponder the possibility that the Bible is not the final word on all subjects, what the New Testament tells us about slavery. In essence, the New Testament writers condone slavery and tell slaves to honor their masters. It also counsels slave owners to treat their slaves with respect, a giant step toward grace in that first-century culture.

But those who advocated slavery in America in the nineteenth century used the Bible to legitimize their claims. If the Bible doesn't outlaw slavery, they reasoned, why should they? Even stronger, if the Bible seems to support slavery, shouldn't they do the same?

But honestly, who among us believes that Paul's admonitions about slavery in Ephesians 6 are the final word on the subject? Don't we read his words today and know that they are conditioned by his slave-oriented culture and his strong desire not to see the church torn apart by a revolution of slaves?

Don't we know that the biblical word on slavery is a valid, even gracious, word for that period, but a word that needed to be expanded over time? And aren't we glad that 1,800 years after Paul wrote his words, slavery was finally abolished in America, and the freedom Paul so coveted became a reality for slaves in our country?

If that is true for the issue of slavery, couldn't it be true for other issues as well? Must we insist that the Bible have the last word on the role of women in the church, parenting wayward teenagers, personal finances, or cures for cancer?

Or can we come to see the Bible as broaching subjects that we, too, need to grapple with, subjects that yield no easy answers in any age? Can we allow the biblical writers to be real people struggling with real issues in their day? Can we learn from them, and then, as with the issue of slavery, see their positions as seeds needing to come to fruition in our time and place?

What if the Bible is not the last word on some important issues, but the first word? What if its purpose is to open the discussion and then let those of us in the church talk, pray, seek the Spirit's wisdom, and come to some reasonable conclusions? Would that destroy the Bible's authority, or would it make the Bible what God intends it to be?

The words of Peter Enns seem relevant here:

> Although the Bible is clear on central matters of faith, it is flexible in many matters that pertain to the day-to-day. To put it more positively, the Bible sets trajectories, not rules, for a good many issues that confront the church. . . . Different people in different contexts will enter into these trajectories in different ways and, therefore, express their commitment to Christ differently. This flexibility of application is precisely what is modeled for us in the pages of Scripture itself.[4]

If we Christians could realize that the Bible doesn't give us the final word on all subjects, we might quit fighting with one another. We might start giving some credence and grace to Christians who have read Scripture and come out at a different place than we have. If it is true that Scripture doesn't have the final word on every topic, that means that we don't have to have the final word either.

Third, *the Bible is not easy to understand.* That desperate father who started reading the Bible through to find an answer to his parenting dilemma assumed three things. First, he assumed that the Bible is a handbook. Second, he assumed that it has definitive answers to questions like how to deal with a stubborn sixteen-year-old. And third, he assumed that it is readily accessible and understandable to anyone who wants to read it. Sadly, he was wrong on all three counts.

As we have seen, the Bible is not a handbook. It also does not give us final answers to all of our questions. And now I am going to add that it is not at all easy to understand. In truth, the Bible is a daunting book that has spawned hundreds of different interpretations of hundreds of different topics. To ever say "this is what Christians believe" is foolish. We Christians have never agreed on even the most basic of doctrines, and yet we all claim to base our beliefs on Scripture.

Think about the issues over which we have battled, split, and formed denominations: the nature of the Bible, divine foreknowledge, the creation of the world, atonement, eternal security, baptism, the Lord's Supper, charismatic gifts, women in ministry, the millennium, hell, war, divorce and remarriage, capital punishment, abortion, homosexuality, and so on and so on, ad infinitum.

If someone were to ask, "What does the Bible say?' about any of these issues, there would be a loud cacophony of conflicting replies. Christians are divided on these issues, and we're all convinced that we, and our church, have the most biblical position of all.

Christian Smith says what we all know but are hesitant to confess:

> On important matters the Bible apparently is not clear, consistent, and univocal enough to enable the best-intentioned, most highly-skilled believing readers to come to agreement as to what it teaches. That is an empirical, historical, undeniable, and ever-present reality. It is, in fact, the single reality that has most shaped the organizational and cultural life of the Christian church, which now, particularly in the United States, exists in a state of massive fragmentation.[5]

*Biblicism* insists that the Bible is consistent, clear, and complete— which sounds good until we actually read the Bible and discover that the Bible is inconsistent, confusing, and ambiguous! The reason

Christianity exists in a state of massive fragmentation is that well-meaning, sincere Christians read the same Bible and come out at very different places.

If that father who started reading through the Bible does manage to keep reading past the Pentateuch, he will eventually find himself asking a host of questions:

• Am I made right with God by my good works or by the grace of God?
• Do I have to be baptized to get salvation?
• What should I do with all of these bizarre Old Testament passages?
• Can women serve as leaders in the church?
• Does God want me to tithe?
• Can I be a Christian and still drink alcohol?
• Is homosexuality a sin?
• Should a Christian ever get an abortion?
• Is God really a Trinity?
• Is the Bible an inerrant word from God?

The longer he reads the Bible, the more questions he will add to his list. If he decides to visit churches to find out what Christians believe about those issues, he will be dismayed at what he discovers.

One church will tell him he has to do good works to make it with God; another will tell him salvation is by grace alone. One church will tell him that he must be baptized to enter into relationship with God; another will tell him baptism is a symbol. One church will tell him he can never take a drink of alcohol; another will tell him that God never commands that we abstain from drinking.

He will discover, in other words, that there is no clear consensus among Christians on these questions, and he might be even more confused after visiting churches than he was before.

That man will discover, in other words, what all of us eventually discover: the Bible is not easy to understand, and sincere Christians will read it and disagree on what it says. Biblicism's claim that the Bible is consistent, clear, and complete just doesn't square with what we see all around us.

# What the Bible Is

So the question then becomes, if the Bible is not a handbook for living, not the answer to all of our questions, and not easy to understand, what exactly is it? What is the Bible's purpose, and how are we to use it? We've considered what the Bible is *not*; it's time to consider what it *is*.

First, *the Bible is a flashlight that points to the Living Word of God.* Scripture is a secondary word, pointing to the first and best Word of God—Jesus Christ. The purpose of the Bible is to focus on Christ— the Old Testament *anticipates* his coming, and the New Testament *celebrates* his coming.

In my book *Making the Good News Good Again*, I have a chapter titled "Is the Bible Good News or Bad?" In that chapter I use this illustration:

> Think of the Bible as a circus, which, if you think about it, is an apt description of it. The Bible is full of color, action, and larger-than-life characters, much like the typical circus. Like the circus, the Bible has sideshows and a center ring. Circus sideshows might include the world's largest man, the world's strongest woman, and other fascinating people and creatures. Scriptural sideshows include the Old Testament stories and laws, which are fascinating and entertaining and make for an interesting read. They also include some of Paul's counsel to specific churches and some of John's wild dreams in the book of Revelation.
>
> But the center ring of attraction of the Bible is Jesus. We pass by those sideshows to make it to the main attraction of the biblical circus: Jesus dying on a cross and then rising from the dead to defeat death. Now that is a main attraction worth seeing! Everything else in the Bible leads us to that center ring, where we get to stand in awe at what God has done for us in Christ. Once we get to the center ring, we understand why the message about Jesus is called good news. Once we get there, we can only be amazed at this miracle that has saved us and set us free.[6]

The Bible is a flashlight that points clearly to Jesus, the Living Word of God, the best revelation of God given to humanity, the center ring in the circus of divine disclosure. And the problem with the handbook approach to Scripture is that it cheapens and obscures that message. If people go to the Bible asking how they should lose weight, make money, or even control their teenage son, they have missed the whole point of Scripture. The Bible is not a book of tips on successful living; it is a book that points to Jesus Christ and says, "Get connected to him."

Once we get connected to him, we will have a gospel frame of reference that has implications for our weight loss, our finances, and our parenting. But the key to understanding Scripture is to know Christ and to have that gospel frame of reference, to soak ourselves in his perspective on life.

That is a different approach to the Bible, though, from the manual-of-life approach most evident in our culture today. It is more indirect than direct, more personal than propositional. And it is always centered on Christ.

A writer named Keith Ward says it well:

> For a Christian, every part of the Bible must in some way point to Christ, to the living person of Jesus who is the Christ and to the unlimited, liberating love of God which is revealed in Christ. To put it bluntly, it is not the words of the Bible that are "the way, the truth, and the life." It is the person of Christ, to whom the Bible witnesses.[7]

If we try to make the Bible into a handbook of human happiness, we trivialize it and obscure its true purpose. If we let it be the flashlight it truly is, it serves quite effectively as a "lamp unto our feet and a light unto our path" (Ps 119:105).

Second, *the Bible is what it is, and we shouldn't try to change it.* Earlier, I wrote that the Bible is inconsistent, confusing, and ambiguous. Frankly, that bothers us a lot. We would prefer to have a divinely dictated book that is consistent, clear, and easy to interpret, so we keep insisting that's what we have. But we don't, and if we truly believe that the Bible is inspired by God, isn't it a bit haughty to reject what we have and try to turn it into something it is not?

I'm reminded of a parent who wanted a child who was beautiful, athletic, and brilliant. But what that parent got was a child who was plain, awkward, and of average intelligence. That parent can be disappointed in the child, or that parent can pretend the child is something she is not, but neither of those approaches will make for a healthy relationship or a healthy child.

What that parent must learn to do is embrace that child as a plain, awkward, reasonably intelligent . . . miracle of God! That child who is a little heavy, clumsy, and dense is an absolute delight. She has a great sense of humor, a heart bigger than Texas, and the capacity to make everyone feel at ease. She is a great kid, if only you have eyes to see her strengths, if only you don't destroy her with your expectations.

And that's the way it is with the Bible. Evidently, this strange book with the bizarre parts that make us cringe, the unreadable sections like Nahum and Zephaniah, and the odd laws and customs of the ancient Jews is precisely the book God wants us to have.

Had God wanted to give us a book spelling out cures for cancer, obesity, or depression, God could have done so. But, for whatever reason, God gave us the Bible we have. And we do not honor God or the Bible if we play make-believe.

So, instead of trying to change it and make it something it isn't, let's embrace the Bible for what it is—a sprawling, difficult, ambiguous compilation of writings that centers on God and what God has done in history, writings that point to Christ and then celebrate Christ.

Let's embrace the fact that not all of the Bible is particularly relevant to our time and place. And let's embrace the fact, too, that some parts of the Bible are conditioned by the beliefs and customs of ancient people—beliefs and customs we no longer find tenable.

In short, let's embrace the Bible as it actually is. But let's not play make-believe and spurn what we have for what we wish we had.

Hear Christian Smith on this topic:

> Regardless of the actual Bible that God has given his church, *biblicists* want a Bible that is different. They want a Bible that answers all their questions, that tells them how to have marital intimacy,

OF AIRPLANES AND SAILBOATS

that gives principles for economics and medicine and science and cooking—and does so inerrantly. They essentially demand—in God's name, yet actually based on a faulty modern philosophy of language and knowledge—a sacred text that will make them certain and secure, though that is not actually the kind of text that God gave.[8]

Most of us probably wish God had given us a different kind of text. It would be nice to have infallible and divine instructions on the specific dilemmas we have to face. I wish I could point that father trying to survive the rebellion of his teenage son to the part of the Bible titled "Ten Tips for Dealing with Your Teenager." I would rather have that in the Bible than Nahum and Zephaniah.

But the Bible is what it is, and, with faith in the sovereignty of God, I accept that. I don't have to know everything. As much as I would like to have divine answers to all the mysteries of life, I can live with uncertainty. I can be grateful for the Bible I do have and trust that God has given me all that I need to know to live with joy and purpose.

Third, *the Bible is an invitation calling us to enter the movement of God in our own time and place.* The Bible is a constant reminder that God is alive and well and working in human history. Even if we don't understand everything in the Bible or agree with everything in the Bible, it underscores the truth that God works in history. God speaks. God judges. God forgives. God is a Factor not to be forgotten. If nothing else, Scripture reminds us that God is active and working in our day, too.

Unfortunately, *biblicism* would have us believe that the Bible is an encyclopedia detailing what God has done in the past and that everything important has already happened.

But what if the Bible is a reminder to us that God is alive, dynamic, and a Factor not to be forgotten in our own time?

What if it reminds us that God is doing a new thing in our day and that we, as God's people, are supposed to discover what that new thing is?

What if the Bible is not just an archive of old truth but an invitation to discover new truth?

What if the Bible serves as a reminder to every generation that God is doing a new and wonderful thing among us, if only we have the wisdom and courage to embrace it?

In short, what if we dared to believe that the same God who spoke centuries ago is still speaking today? And what if we let the Bible nudge us to hear the Spirit's message to us—a fresh, vibrant message that can set our hearts on fire?

## Back to the Bible

My father's favorite radio program was "Back to the Bible," and he listened to it almost every day. I never listened to that program as much as he did, but I find myself now wishing we could get "back to the Bible." I wish we could return to the Bible as it really is. I wish we could escape the tenets of *biblicism* so the Bible could be what it is supposed to be.

Frankly, I worry about those who cling to *biblicism*. Those who have the handbook view of Scripture, who think the Bible has an infallible word to say on all topics, and who believe that everyone can comprehend the tenets of Scripture will eventually grow disillusioned. They will discover that those things are not true and not know what to do with their discovery.

Young people will abandon the Bible because they see it as foreign to their own experience. Weary parents, like the father I described, will abandon the Bible because they see it as irrelevant to their parenting problems. Earnest seekers will abandon the Bible because they can't comprehend what it is saying. Even long-time Christians will abandon the Bible because they're frustrated with *biblicism* but have nothing else to put in its place.

But the problem is not with the Bible. The problem is with our approach to the Bible. The problem is that we've bought into the tenets of *biblicism* and made the Bible into something it is not supposed to be. The problem is that we've been building an airplane when what we actually have is a sailboat.

OF AIRPLANES AND SAILBOATS

Once we realize it's a sailboat we're building, we might be able to put it together with delight and appreciate it more than we ever have. Once we let the Bible point us toward Christ, be the amazing and confounding book it really is, and offer us the invitation to hear God in our own day, we might begin to see the Bible as the God-given resource it actually is. We might quit worrying about the Bible and fighting over the Bible . . . and start loving the Bible.

## For Reflection or Discussion

1. Do you agree with the author's premise that we typically misuse the Bible? Are we trying to build an airplane when what we really have is a sailboat?

2. Did you grow up with *biblicism*? How many of the ten assumptions of *biblicism* were you taught to believe?

3. Do you sympathize with that father trying to guide his teenage son and looking to the Bible for help? What would you say to that father? And how would you explain the Leviticus passage to him?

4. Are you comfortable with the notion that God never intended us to have direct, specific, nonnegotiable instructions on everything? Does that idea destroy the Bible's authority for you or enhance it?

5. Is it heresy to assert that the Bible is not clear, consistent, or univocal enough to lead to Christian consensus? Or is it honest and helpful to assert that?

6. What would it mean to our faith if we accepted the Bible just as it is—a sprawling, difficult, ambiguous compilation of writings that center on God and what God has done through Jesus Christ? Would we be more open and accepting of those who disagree with our interpretations of it?

# Notes

1. Christian Smith, *The Bible Made Impossible,* digital version (Grand Rapids: Brazos Press, 2011) location 208.

2. Ibid., location 2471.

3. Ibid., location 2298.

4. Peter Enns, *Inspiration and Incarnation* (Grand Rapids: Baker Academic, 2005) 170.

5. Smith, *The Bible Made Impossible,* location 662.

6. Judson Edwards, *Making the Good News Good Again* (Macon GA: Smyth & Helwys, 2009) 45–46.

7. Keith Ward, *What the Bible Really Teaches* (London: SPCK, 2004) 27.

8. Smith, *The Bible Made Impossible,* location 2604–605.

# CHAPTER 8

# Quiet Faith
*(How Can I Fashion a Quiet Faith in a Loud World?)*

Every book is an invitation to take a journey, and every author is a tour guide. The books we love the most are the ones that take us on a grand adventure, and the authors we love the most are the ones who prove to be interesting and entertaining guides on that adventure.

When we began this book, I invited you take a trip with me, a trip to consider some important facets of a life with God. The journey we were going to take was a spiritual one, probing the depths of our minds and souls.

I confessed early on that I was a tour guide much influenced by a number of factors. I confessed that I am a Christian, a Baptist, an introvert, a retired pastor, and something of an evangelical misfit.

Each of those factors has affected my perspective of the world, God, and all of the topics I've addressed in this book. My angle on the world is not an infallible one, for sure, but it is the only one I have, and I have enjoyed sharing it with you. If nothing else, you have learned how one Christian-Baptist-introvert-retired pastor-misfit sees the truth.

If you have stayed with me this long, the chances are good that you share at least some of my views. Had you been of a radically different persuasion, you would have quit this book long ago and searched for something more conservative, liberal, uplifting, extroverted, prophetic, humorous, or whatever.

The fact that you've made it to the last chapter of the book says you are probably something of a kindred spirit. It's encouraging to me to know that there is at least one of you out there!

But I also know that fashioning a quiet faith in a loud world can be lonely and discouraging work. It's easy to join the "popular religion" crowd, but that way leads to shallow faith and, ultimately, disillusionment. And it's easy to join the haughty nonreligious crowd, but that way leads to cynicism and despair.

Somewhere between those extremes is an honest, quiet faith that takes God seriously, prompts us to serve other people, and leads us to a life of joy and purpose. Somewhere between popular religion and no religion at all is a way that leads to what Jesus called "abundant life" (John 10:10).

But finding that way requires both wisdom and perseverance—the wisdom to find the truth and then the perseverance to keep following that truth. It is, at times, a lonely journey, because we quiet Christians typically don't like to join groups and "share our feelings." We tend to get by ourselves, read books, and think things through. We like to be alone, but sometimes "alone" can become "lonely."

In this final chapter, I'd like to offer you what I hope are some practical suggestions for building a quiet faith in a world of hustle and hype. See these suggestions as travel tips from a kindred spirit.

## Travel Tips from a Kindred Spirit

Here are seven truths I think are especially important to those of us who are quiet, reflective Christians.

*Assume that the narrow road is the best road.* The two roads I just mentioned are broad, well traveled, and easy to see.

On one road, the haughty, nonreligious crowd scoffs at faith of any kind and is convinced that God is either nonexistent or unknowable. The tribe of Secular Man is growing and vocal, and that road is getting more crowded every day.

But the road of popular religion is getting crowded, too. The number of people hooked on religious clichés and shallow truth is both staggering and discouraging. Sadly, Secular Man has justifiable reasons to scoff at what many modern Christians say and do.

Those two groups heading down those two congested roads give a whole new meaning to Jesus' injunction in the Sermon on the

Mount to walk a narrow road. Somewhere between the cynicism of the unbelieving crowd and the shallowness of the believing crowd is a narrow road of honest faith.

It's the road I want to be on, though I know it will not be a popular road to travel. If I travel the narrow road, the secularists will call me a fool, the fundamentalists will call me a heretic, and I will be welcomed in neither camp.

But I do believe the narrow road is the best road to travel. When I look at where those other roads lead, I don't think I want to go there. When I look around me, I know that the status quo is not particularly impressive. You don't have to be a prophet or a genius to notice that our world is in bad shape and that both secularism and fundamentalism are dead-end streets.

John Meagher writes,

> We must—repeat, *must*—shed our acculturated and perversely uncircumspect assumption that we live in a smart world. We are victims of its dumbest recorded state. Once we realize that we are the crippled products of an extraordinarily stupid, insensitive, selfish, blind, and self-deceived moment in history, we can get on with what needs to be done about it; but until then, we are likely to compound its dizzying insanity. If you have managed to reach ten, for God's sake don't accept the constant invitation to slip back to five, which is nowhere, or six, which is uncomfortable collusion with collective atrocities.[1]

Look around. Is this the best we can do? Is this the best we Christians can think and act and live? Is the broad road of popular religion going to change our world and give it depth and substance? Or is popular religion merely a symptom of the problem? And is a retreat into secularism the answer? Will that take us to depth and substance?

I think it safe to assume that neither popular religion nor secularism can get us where we want, and need, to be. So let's get on a narrow road and see where it takes us.

*Keep getting rid of your gods.* Earlier I quoted John Meagher, who said he had believed, and then discarded, approximately thirty-seven different editions of God. I'm not sure I've had that many Gods, but I've had my share.

Over my lifetime, I've believed in, and then discarded, at least these editions of God:

• *The Vengeful God*, who ruled in the Old Testament and who, even in our day, exacts revenge on all who fail to measure up to his standards.

• *The Magical God*, who rewards people for doing superstitious things, like crossing themselves while they're standing in the batter's box, reading the Bible every morning, or putting a statue on their dashboard.

• *The Slot Machine God*, who bestows blessings on people if they are persistent enough in putting their prayer coins in the slot.

• *The Dogmatic God*, who demands that I believe in him without ever questioning or thinking "outside the box."

• *The Disappointed God*, who wants me to be some things I'm not— loud, brash, certain, and extroverted, to mention just a few.

• *The Vocal God*, who will one day thunder edicts from heaven, bowl me over with a blinding light, or in some other way reveal himself to me.

• *The Powerful God*, who rules with obvious right-handed power instead of the more subtle left-handed power—"the power of the cross," as Paul puts it.

• *The Reluctant God*, who must be begged and besieged before he will answer prayers and grant requests.

• *The Limited God*, who can allow into his presence only people like me—evangelical Protestants (preferably Baptist) who have the correct theology.

There have probably been others, but, suffice it to say, I've had many Gods in my life. Years ago, J. B. Phillips wrote a book titled *Your God Is Too Small*, and he was right.[2] My God was too small and still is too small. So I'm eager to see what new truths I will discover about God in the days ahead.

*Embrace a God who loves truth.* Jesus gave all of us who are searchers and questioners permission to probe when he said, "You will know the truth, and the truth will make you free" (John 8:32).

Another name for God is Truth. We never have to be afraid of truth, for when we discover truth we have found God. Wherever we discover truth—in the Bible, in a microscope, in our own experience, or in the heart and life of another person, let's celebrate it and know that we are standing on holy ground.

Let's ask, seek, and knock with confidence and passion. Let's pursue truth whenever and wherever we can find it. And whenever and wherever we do find it, let's whisper a prayer of gratitude that we are in the presence of God.

*Lean into your doubts.* I do believe that doubts are the ants in the pants of faith. Without doubts, we are destined *not* to move. We will continue in the same rut all of our days, never discovering new truth, never probing new ideas, never meeting new people. I shudder to think where I would be theologically and emotionally if I hadn't doubted some of the treasured truths I grew up with.

The only way up the ladder of personal maturity is by doubting and becoming disillusioned with the rung of the ladder on which we currently stand. Certainly, we will never "get there." We will never understand God, comprehend life's mysteries, or become completely mature and finished human beings.

But the joy of living is the joy of moving up the ladder. And, as I said, the only way to do that is to doubt and probe and become a misfit—at least to the people who are on the same rung of that ladder as we are.

*Lean into your convictions.* I think it is important that we balance our doubts with our convictions. True, we don't know everything and need to be honest enough to admit it. But it is also true that we do have some convictions, some foundational truths that undergird our faith and make us Christian.

Those of us who, by nature, tend to be quiet, reflective, brooding types especially need to "circle the wagons" from time to time and remind ourselves of the basic truths that hold our lives together. We can easily drown in skepticism and cynicism if we're not careful, so, to balance ourselves, we need to affirm the things we *do* believe.

That's why I put early in this book a chapter on "Reclaiming the Center" and mentioned to you four foundational pillars in my own life—GRACE, FAITH, GRATITUDE, and HUMILITY. On those four truths, I can build a life that I think is both biblical and honest.

On the days when doubts assail me and God seems far, far away, I cling to those convictions like a drowning man clutching a life preserver. I will not let doubt have the final word. I will only let doubt nudge me into truer convictions and a more resolute focus on the things that matter.

*Remember that your joy is more important than your theology.* The ultimate test of our faith in God is not our theology, our doctrinal correctness, or our observance of religious rituals and services. The ultimate test of our faith in God is our joy. They will know we are Christians by our love, for sure, but they will also know we are Christians by our joy.

I have observed a number of church people through the years who were grounded in biblical truth, faithful in church attendance, and models of morality and virtue. But some of them were mean-spirited. Some were angry. Some were bored with life. They seemed to observe all of the religious principles we Christians teach and treasure, but they didn't have the joy those principles are supposed to produce. The "means," somehow, never led to the "ends."

I have also observed a number of people who are not particularly religious and seldom, if ever, darken the doors of a church. But these people are full of life, laughter, and wonder. In their presence, I have come alive, too, for their joy is contagious. And I have thought, on more than one occasion, that these nonreligious people are closer to the kingdom than my mean-spirited, angry, bored church friends. Wherever there is joy, I have concluded, there is the presence of God.

Our preoccupation with doctrinal correctness can blind us to the truth that joy is the most infallible proof of the presence of God. Even our desire to be "more open," "more liberal," and "more accepting" than our fellow Christians can blind us to that truth.

The surest sign that we know God, and the best way to influence the world for God, is to live a life that overflows with delight.

*Be true to the difference to which you have been created and called.* In the front of her book *Quiet,* Susan Cain has this quote from Alan Shawn:

> A species in which everyone was General Patton would not succeed, any more than would a race in which everyone was Vincent van Gogh. I prefer to think that the planet needs athletes, philosophers, sex symbols, painters, scientists; it needs the warmhearted, the hard-hearted, the coldhearted, and the weakhearted. It needs those who can devote their lives to studying how many droplets of water are secreted by the salivary glands of dogs under which circumstances, and it needs those who can capture the passing impression of cherry blossoms in a fourteen-syllable poem or devote twenty-five pages to the dissection of a small boy's feelings as he lies in bed in the dark waiting for his mother to kiss him goodnight.[3]

We're all different, all needed, and all stuck with the way we're glued together. But we can learn to admit our weaknesses and, at the same time, enjoy and use our strengths.

Those of us who possess the weaknesses and strengths of an introvert will have to work hard to enjoy and use our strengths. As I mentioned, the church consistently holds up extroversion to us as the way Jesus was and the way we ought to be.

Adam McHugh says,

> The evangelical culture ties together faithfulness and extroversion. The emphasis is on community, on participating in more and more programs and events, on meeting more and more people. It's a con-stant tension for many introverts that they're not living that out. And in a religious world, there's more at stake when you feel that tension. It doesn't feel like "I'm not doing as well as I'd like." It feels like "God isn't pleased with me."[4]

That is the way we sometimes feel. We feel that God can't possibly be pleased with a quiet, reflective, brooding wallflower who enjoys being alone and cringes at the thought of "group activities." We hope and pray that one day we'll "come out of our shell" and become extroverts.

To put it bluntly: That's not going to happen. We're going to have to embrace who we are and be true to the difference to which we have been created and called. Let's embrace our love of solitude, creativity, and thinking; our willingness to play the role of an extrovert when we have to; our desire to find the truth, even if it is not popular; our loyalty to our friends and family; our genuine appreciation for little things and small blessings; our willingness to work behind the scenes to make things happen; our love of privacy; our hunger for God and truth and honesty; and all of the other weird and wonderful qualities that make introverts indispensable.

If we happen to have those qualities, let's count our blessings. Let's realize, too, that it would be an affront to the God who made us to wish we were anything but who we are. The planet doesn't need everyone to be General Patton or Vincent van Gogh, and the planet doesn't need everyone to be an in-your-face, aggressive Christian either. I'm convinced that the planet needs a host of quiet, reflective Christians like you and me.

## A Biblical Mandate

Evidently, the Apostle Paul thought so, too. In his first letter to Timothy, Paul, who usually comes across in the Bible as anything but a quiet Christian, offered some counsel to Timothy that is a manifesto for all of us who tend to be quiet and reflective in our faith:

> First of all, then, I urge that supplications, prayers, intercessions, and thanksgivings be made for everyone, for kings and all who are in high positions, so that we may lead a quiet and peaceable life in all godliness and dignity. This is right and is acceptable in the sight of God our Savior, who desires everyone to be saved and to come to the knowledge of the truth. (1 Tim 2:1-4)

How do we change the world? And by that I mean the world in which we actually live, the small world of our family, friends, church, and work. How do we make a positive difference in the context of our marriage, parenting, church life, and work life? What do we need to do to make a difference right where we are?

Paul says it begins with an attitude: "I urge that supplications, prayers, intercessions, and thanksgivings be made for everyone, for kings and all who are in high positions. . . ." Just reading that enables us to sense the spirit Paul has in mind. We are to pray for everyone, especially kings and those in high positions.

That last line is especially striking. It is generally believed that when Paul wrote First Timothy, Nero was the emperor of Rome. Nero was certainly not a model of virtue and goodness, to say the least. But Paul says to pray for him anyway and for all who are in leadership positions.

There is a grace and generosity here that shows us the kind of attitude that changes a marriage, blesses a child, makes an office more loving, and makes church a community. It's a spirit that is not mean and critical, but kind and loving. This gracious, "pray-for-everyone" attitude sets the stage for changing the world.

Then, once he sets that attitude in place, Paul gets down to the specifics of how to be a creative change agent in the world: "that we may lead a quiet and peaceable life in all godliness and dignity." He uses four words to describe the kind of person who makes a positive difference in the world.

First, this person is *quiet*. In contrast to our culture's insistence that we have to make a lot of noise to get noticed and make a difference, Paul recommends a quiet life. He is describing a life that calls no attentions to itself, makes no unnecessary racket, and is not into flash and dazzle at all.

Second, this person is *peaceable*. This person's life is marked by peace—peaceful relationships, peaceful emotions, peace with God. When people are filled with peace, good things happen all around them. They provide an atmosphere in which others can flourish. There's something about peace that is contagious and affects a whole system.

Third, this person is *godly*. Paul uses this word eight times in First Timothy alone. It describes a person whose life is centered on God, focused on God, soaked in God. This is a person who worships, prays, studies, and allows God to operate as God. This is a person so focused on God that he or she starts to love the way God loves.

Fourth, this person has *dignity*. The biblical translators struggled with this fourth characteristic. The RSV translators used the word "dignity," but other translators used "holiness," "honesty," "reverence," and "gravity" to capture this quality. Whichever word we opt for, the idea is the same: this is a person willing to be different, comfortable in his or her own skin, and exuding a quiet confidence. Whichever word we use, this is a person willing to be true to the difference to which he or she has been called.

Put those four qualities together, and we can picture the kind of person Paul is describing: a quiet, peaceable, godly, dignified person. But when we read those adjectives, we're prone to think, "That sounds like a nice person, all right, but that person won't make much of a mark in the real world. There's not enough flash and sizzle in that life. It's *too* quiet, peaceable, godly, and dignified to be noticed. That person is much too wimpy to make much of a difference in our kind of culture."

You can almost sense that Paul is reading our minds, though. It's as if he knows we're going to object. So he says that this attitude of praying for everyone and being quiet, peaceable, godly, and dignified is precisely God's plan for changing the world: "This is right and is acceptable in the sight of God our Savior, who desires everyone to be saved and to come to the knowledge of the truth."

According to Paul, people who pray for everyone and who live lives that are quiet, peaceable, godly, and dignified will be the very people who *do* change the world. It is good, he says, when people live this way because God wants everyone to be saved and to come to a knowledge of the truth. These quiet, peaceable, godly, and dignified people are the best beacons for others to follow if they want to find the Truth.

But we don't just have to take Paul's word for that. When we look at our own experience, we realize that the people who have influenced us the most and led us to faith in God are people just like the ones Paul describes in these verses in First Timothy.

At least for me, the people who have changed my life have not been loud, aggressive, and noticed by the masses. The people who have changed my life have been quiet, peaceful, centered on God, and willing to be true to the difference to which they have been called. Those are the people who have changed my life, so it's impossible for me to argue with Paul.

Are we really attracted to people who are loud, pushing their cause, and trying to sell us something? Are those the kinds of people who change us? Or are we drawn to people who are quiet, genuine, and gracious—people flying "under the radar" in our culture? When we think about our own experience, I think most of us would say that Paul is right on target in this passage.

If I asked you, "What does an evangelist look like?" many of you would have an image come to mind. You think of an evangelist as someone who is loud, dogmatic, colorful, and bold. If you grew up in the "revival era," as I did, you might even conjure up an image of a man wearing a bright suit and screaming from a pulpit. Sadly, the word "evangelist" has negative connotations for most people in our society.

Let's get a new image of an evangelist. In light of this passage in First Timothy, let's think of an evangelist as a quiet, peaceable person who loves God and dares to be different. But even more to the point, let's realize that an evangelist—the kind of person who makes a positive difference in the world—could look just like us.

We don't have to be loud. We don't have to be pushy. And we don't have to make headlines. We can be quiet people, living peacefully with God and others. We can fashion an honest faith and dare to live out that faith in specific ways in the world.

Praise God, we can be ourselves. We can be introverts. We can be misfits. And, lo and behold, we can also be evangelists, quietly making a difference where we live and love.

## For Reflection or Discussion

1. Is building a quiet faith in a loud world lonely and discouraging work for you? Why or why not?

2. Are you most tempted by the popular religion crowd, or the secular, nonreligious crowd? How do you manage to stay on the narrow road between those two extremes?

3. Do you agree that we are not living in a smart world and that something needs to change? How can we quietly challenge the stupidity of the status quo?

4. How many Gods have you had in your life? Which ones were you especially glad to get rid of?

5. If joy is more important than theology, how do we get more of it? What gives you your greatest joy?

6. Have you known joyless believers and joyful unbelievers? How do you explain that?

7. When you look back at your life, what kinds of people have influenced you most? What does that tell you about the kind of person you need to be to influence others?

8. Can we really be ourselves and quietly change the world? How?

## NOTES

1. John Meagher, *The Truing of Christianity* (New York: Doubleday, 1990) 256.

2. J. B. Phillips, *Your God Is Too Small* (New York: Macmillan, 1953).

3. Susan Cain, *Quiet* (New York: Crown, 2012) front matter.

4. Quoted in Cain, *Quiet*, 66.

*Other available titles from*

---

## Beyond the American Dream
*Millard Fuller*

In 1968, Millard finished the story of his journey from pauper to millionaire to home builder. His wife, Linda, occasionally would ask him about getting it published, but Millard would reply, "Not now. I'm too busy." This is that story.   *978-1-57312-563-5  272 pages/pb  $20.00*

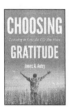

## Blissful Affliction
### The Ministry and Misery of Writing
*Judson Edwards*

Edwards draws from more than forty years of writing experience to explore why we use the written word to change lives and how to improve the writing craft.   *978-1-57312-594-9  144 pages/pb  $15.00*

## Choosing Gratitude
### Learning to Love the Life You Have
*James A. Autry*

Autry reminds us that gratitude is a choice, a spiritual—not social—process. He suggests that if we cultivate gratitude as a way of being, we may not change the world and its ills, but we can change our response to the world. If we fill our lives with moments of gratitude, we will indeed love the life we have.   *978-1-57312-614-4  144 pages/pb  $15.00*

## Contextualizing the Gospel
### A Homiletic Commentary on 1 Corinthians
*Brian L. Harbour*

Harbour examines every part of Paul's letter, providing a rich resource for those who want to struggle with the difficult texts as well as the simple texts, who want to know how God's word—all of it—intersects with their lives today.   *978-1-57312-589-5  240 pages/pb  $19.00*

## Dance Lessons
### Moving to the Beat of God's Heart
*Jeanie Miley*

Miley shares her joys and struggles a she learns to "dance" with the Spirit of the Living God.   *978-1-57312-622-9  240 pages/pb  $19.00*

To order call **1-800-747-3016** or visit **www.helwys.com**

## Daniel (Smyth & Helwys Annual Bible Study series)
### Keeping Faith When the Heat Is On
*Bill Ireland*

Daniel is a book about resistance. It was written to people under pressure. In the book, we will see the efforts oppressive regimes take to undermine the faith and identity of God's people. In it, we will also see the strategies God's people employed in resisting the imposition of a foreign culture, and we will see what sustained their efforts. In that vein, the book of Daniel is powerfully relevant. *Teaching Guide 978-1-57312-647-2 144 pages/pb* **$14.00**

*Study Guide 978-1-57312-646-5 80 pages/pb* **$6.00**

## A Divine Duet
### Ministry and Motherhood
*Alicia Davis Porterfield, ed.*

Each essay in this inspiring collection is as different as the mother-minister who wrote it, from theologians to chaplains, inner-city ministers to rural-poverty ministers, youth pastors to preachers, mothers who have adopted, birthed, and done both.

*978-1-57312-676-2 146 pages/pb* **$16.00**

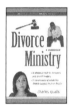

## Divorce Ministry
### A Guidebook
*Charles Qualls*

This book shares with the reader the value of establishing a divorce recovery ministry while also offering practical insights on establishing your own unique church-affiliated program. Whether you are working individually with one divorced person or leading a large group, *Divorce Ministry: A Guidebook* provides helpful resources to guide you through the emotional and relational issues divorced people often encounter.

*978-1-57312-588-8 156 pages/pb* **$16.00**

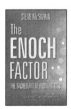

## The Enoch Factor
### The Sacred Art of Knowing God
*Steve McSwain*

*The Enoch Factor* is a persuasive argument for a more enlightened religious dialogue in America, one that affirms the goals of all religions—guiding followers in self-awareness, finding serenity and happiness, and discovering what the author describes as "the sacred art of knowing God." *978-1-57312-556-7 256 pages/pb* **$21.00**

### Healing Our Hurts
Coping with Difficult Emotions

*Daniel Bagby*

In *Healing Our Hurts*, Daniel Bagby identifies and explains all the dynamics at play in these complex emotions. Offering practical biblical insights to these feelings, he interprets faith-based responses to separate overly religious piety from true, natural human emotion. This book helps us learn how to deal with life's difficult emotions in a redemptive and responsible way.  *978-1-57312-613-7  144 pages/pb* **$15.00**

### Hope for the Thinking Christian
Seeking a Path of Faith through Everyday Life

*Stephen Reese*

Readers who want to confront their faith more directly, to think it through and be open to God in an individual, authentic, spiritual encounter will find a resonant voice in Stephen Reese.

*978-1-57312-553-6  160 pages/pb* **$16.00**

### A Hungry Soul Desperate to Taste God's Grace
Honest Prayers for Life

*Charles Qualls*

Part of how we *see* God is determined by how we *listen* to God. There is so much noise and movement in the world that competes with images of God. This noise would drown out God's beckoning voice and distract us. Charles Qualls's newest book offers readers prayers for that journey toward the meaning and mystery of God.  *978-1-57312-648-9  152 pages/pb* **$14.00**

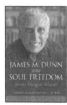

### James M. Dunn and Soul Freedom
*Aaron Douglas Weaver*

James Milton Dunn, over the last fifty years, has been the most aggressive Baptist proponent for religious liberty in the United States. Soul freedom—voluntary, uncoerced faith and an unfettered individual conscience before God—is the basis of his understanding of church-state separation and the historic Baptist basis of religious liberty.

*978-1-57312-590-1  224 pages/pb* **$18.00**

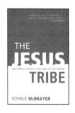

### The Jesus Tribe
Following Christ in the Land of the Empire

*Ronnie McBrayer*

*The Jesus Tribe* fleshes out the implications, possibilities, contradictions, and complexities of what it means to live within the Jesus Tribe and in the shadow of the American Empire.

*978-1-57312-592-5  208 pages/pb* **$17.00**

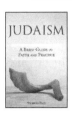

### Judaism
A Brief Guide to Faith and Practice

*Sharon Pace*

Sharon Pace's newest book is a sensitive and comprehensive introduction to Judaism. What is it like to be born into the Jewish community? How does belief in the One God and a universal morality shape the way in which Jews see the world? How does one find meaning in life and the courage to endure suffering? How does one mark joy and forge community ties? *978-1-57312-644-1 144 pages/pb $16.00*

### Lessons from the Cloth 2
501 More One Minute Motivators for Leaders

*Bo Prosser and Charles Qualls*

As the force that drives organizations to accomplishment, leadership is at a crucial point in churches, corporations, families, and almost every arena of life. Without leadership there is chaos. *With* leadership there is sometimes chaos! In this follow-up to their first volume, Bo Prosser and Charles Qualls will inspire you to keep growing in your leadership career. *978-1-57312-665-6 152 pages/pb $11.00*

### Let Me More of Their Beauty See
Reading Familiar Verses in Context

*Diane G. Chen*

*Let Me More of Their Beauty See* offers eight examples of how attention to the historical and literary settings can safeguard against taking a text out of context, bring out its transforming power in greater dimension, and help us apply Scripture appropriately in our daily lives.

*978-1-57312-564-2 160 pages/pb $17.00*

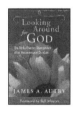

### Looking Around for God
The Strangely Reverent Observations of an Unconventional Christian

*James A. Autry*

*Looking Around for God*, Autry's tenth book, is in many ways his most personal. In it he considers his unique life of faith and belief in God. Autry is a former Fortune 500 executive, author, poet, and consultant whose work has had a significant influence on leadership thinking.

*978-157312-484-3 144 pages/pb $16.00*

## Maggie Lee for Good

*Jinny and John Hinson*

*Maggie Lee for Good* captures the essence of a young girl's boundless faith and spirit. Her parents' moving story of the accident that took her life will inspire readers who are facing loss, looking for evidence of God's sustaining grace, or searching for ways to make a meaningful difference in the lives of others.  *978-1-57312-630-4 144 pages/pb* **$15.00**

## Making the Timeless Word Timely

A Primer for Preachers

*Michael B. Brown*

Michael Brown writes, "There is a simple formula for sermon preparation that creates messages that apply and engage whether your parish is rural or urban, young or old, rich or poor, five thousand members or fifty." The other part of the task, of course, involves being creative and insightful enough to know how to take the general formula for sermon preparation and make it particular in its impact on a specific congregation. Brown guides the reader through the formula and the skills to employ it with excellence and integrity.  *978-1-57312-578-9 160 pages/pb* **$16.00**

## Meeting Jesus Today

For the Cautious, the Curious, and the Committed

*Jeanie Miley*

*Meeting Jesus Today*, ideal for both individual study and small groups, is intended to be used as a workbook. It is designed to move readers from studying the Scriptures and ideas within the chapters to recording their journey with the Living Christ.

*978-1-57312-677-9 320 pages/pb* **$19.00**

## The Ministry Life

101 Tips for New Ministers

*John Killinger*

Sharing years of wisdom from more than fifty years in ministry and teaching, *The Ministry Life: 101 Tips for New Ministers* by John Killinger is filled with practical advice and wisdom for a minister's day-to-day tasks as well as advice on intellectual and spiritual habits to keep ministers of any age healthy and fulfilled.  *978-1-57312-662-5 244 pages/pb* **$19.00**

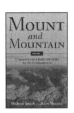

## Mount and Mountain
### Vol. 1: A Reverend and a Rabbi Talk About the Ten Commandments
*Rami Shapiro and Michael Smith*

*Mount and Mountain* represents the first half of an interfaith dialogue—a dialogue that neither preaches nor placates but challenges its participants to work both singly and together in the task of reinterpreting sacred texts. Mike and Rami discuss the nature of divinity, the power of faith, the beauty of myth and story, the necessity of doubt, the achievements, failings, and future of religion, and, above all, the struggle to live ethically and in harmony with the way of God.   *978-1-57312-612-0 144 pages/pb* **$15.00**

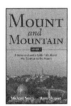

## Mount and Mountain
### Vol. 2: A Reverend and a Rabbi Talk About the Sermon on the Mount
*Rami Shapiro and Michael Smith*

This book, focused on the Sermon on the Mount, represents the second half of Mike and Rami's dialogue. In it, Mike and Rami explore the text of Jesus' sermon cooperatively, contributing perspectives drawn from their lives and religious traditions and seeking moments of illumination.   *978-1-57312-654-0 254 pages/pb* **$19.00**

## Overcoming Adolescence
### Growing Beyond Childhood into Maturity
*Marion D. Aldridge*

In *Overcoming Adolescence*, Marion Aldridge poses questions for adults of all ages to consider. His challenge to readers is one he has personally worked to confront: to grow up *all the way*—mentally, physically, academically, socially, emotionally, and spiritually. The key involves not only knowing how to work through the process but also how to recognize what may be contributing to our perpetual adolescence.

*978-1-57312-577-2 156 pages/pb* **$17.00**

## Psychic Pancakes & Communion Pizza
### More Musings and Mutterings of a Church Misfit
*Bert Montgomery*

*Psychic Pancakes & Communion Pizza* is Bert Montgomery's highly anticipated follow-up to *Elvis, Willie, Jesus & Me* and contains further reflections on music, film, culture, life, and finding Jesus in the midst of it all.   *978-1-57312-578-9 160 pages/pb* **$16.00**

To order call **1-800-747-3016** or visit **www.helwys.com**

## Quiet Faith
### An Introvert's Guide to Spiritual Survival
*Judson Edwards*

In eight finely crafted chapters, Edwards look at key issues like evangelism, interpreting the Bible, dealing with doubt, and surviving the church from the perspective of a confirmed, but sometimes reluctant, introvert. In the process, he offers some provocative insights that introverts will find helpful and reassuring. *978-1-57312-681-6 144 pages/pb* **$15.00**

## Reading Ezekiel (Reading the Old Testament series)
### A Literary and Theological Commentary
*Marvin A. Sweeney*

The book of Ezekiel points to the return of YHWH to the holy temple at the center of a reconstituted Israel and creation at large. As such, the book of Ezekiel portrays the purging of Jerusalem, the Temple, and the people, to reconstitute them as part of a new creation at the conclusion of the book. With Jerusalem, the Temple, and the people so purged, YHWH stands once again in the holy center of the created world.

*978-1-57312-658-8 264 pages/pb* **$22.00**

## Reading Job (Reading the Old Testament series)
### A Literary and Theological Commentary
*James L. Crenshaw*

At issue in the Book of Job is a question with which most all of us struggle at some point in life, "Why do bad things happen to good people?" James Crenshaw has devoted his life to studying the disturbing matter of theodicy—divine justice—that troubles many people of faith.

*978-1-57312-574-1 192 pages/pb* **$22.00**

## Reading Judges (Reading the Old Testament series)
### A Literary and Theological Commentary
*Mark E. Biddle*

Reading the Old Testament book of Judges presents a number of significant challenges related to social contexts, historical settings, and literary characteristics. Acknowledging and examining these difficulties provides a point of entry into the world of Judges and promises to enrich the reading experience. *978-1-57312-631-1 240 pages/pb* **$22.00**

## Reading Samuel (Reading the Old Testament series)
### A Literary and Theological Commentary
*Johanna W. H. van Wijk-Bos*

Interpreted masterfully by preeminent Old Testament scholar Johanna W. H. van Wijk-Bos, the story of Samuel touches on a vast array of subjects that make up the rich fabric of human life. The reader gains an inside look at leadership, royal intrigue, military campaigns, occult practices, and the significance of religious objects of veneration.

978-1-57312-607-6  272 pages/pb  **$22.00**

## The Role of the Minister in a Dying Congregation
*Lynwood B. Jenkins*

Jenkins provides a courageous and responsible resource on one of the most critical issues in congregational life: how to help a congregation conclude its ministry life cycle with dignity and meaning.

978-1-57312-571-0  96 pages/pb  **$14.00**

## Sessions with Genesis (Session Bible Studies series)
### The Story Begins
*Tony W. Cartledge*

Immersing us in the book of Genesis, Tony Cartledge examines both its major stories and the smaller cycles of hope and failure, of promise and judgment. Genesis introduces these themes of divine faithfulness and human failure in unmistakable terms, tracing Israel's beginning to the creation of the world and professing a belief that Israel's particular history had universal significance.

978-1-57312-636-6  144 pages/pb  **$14.00**

## Sessions with Philippians (Session Bible Studies series)
### Finding Joy in Community
*Bo Prosser*

In this brief letter to the Philippians, Paul makes clear the centrality of his faith in Jesus Christ, his love for the Philippian church, and his joy in serving both Christ and their church.

978-1-57312-579-6  112 pages/pb  **$13.00**

## Sessions with Samuel (Session Bible Studies series)
### Stories from the Edge
*Tony W. Cartledge*

In these stories, Israel faces one crisis after another, a people constantly on the edge. Individuals such as Saul and David find themselves on the edge as well, facing troubles of leadership and personal struggle. Yet, each crisis becomes a gateway for learning that God is always present, that hope remains.

978-1-57312-555-0  112 pages/pb  **$13.00**

## Silver Linings
My Life Before and After Challenger 7

*June Scobee Rodgers*

We know the public story of *Challenger 7*'s tragic destruction. That day, June's life took a new direction that ultimately led to the creation of the Challenger Center and to new life and new love. Her story of Christian faith and triumph over adversity will inspire readers of every age.
*978-1-57312-570-3 352 pages/hc* **$28.00**

## Spacious
Exploring Faith and Place

*Holly Sprink*

Exploring where we are and why that matters to God is an ongoing process. If we are present and attentive, God creatively and continuously widens our view of the world, whether we live in the Amazon or in our own hometown.
*978-1-57312-649-6 156 pages/pb* **$16.00**

## This Is What a Preacher Looks Like
Sermons by Baptist Women in Ministry

*Pamela Durso, ed.*

In this collection of sermons by thirty-six Baptist women, their voices are soft and loud, prophetic and pastoral, humorous and sincere. They are African American, Asian, Latina, and Caucasian. They are sisters, wives, mothers, grandmothers, aunts, and friends.
*978-1-57312-554-3 144 pages/pb* **$18.00**

## Transformational Leadership
Leading with Integrity

*Charles B. Bugg*

"Transformational" leadership involves understanding and growing so that we can help create positive change in the world. This book encourages leaders to be willing to change if *they* want to help transform the world. They are honest about their personal strengths and weaknesses, and are not afraid of doing a fearless moral inventory of themselves.
*978-1-57312-558-1 112 pages/pb* **$14.00**

Made in the USA
San Bernardino, CA
04 March 2014